World Bolshevism

World
Bolshevism

Iulii
Martov

In a new translation by
Paul Kellogg and Mariya Melentyeva

With an introduction by Paul Kellogg

AU PRESS

Published by AU Press, Athabasca University
1200, 10011 – 109 Street, Edmonton, AB T5J 3S8

https://doi.org/10.15215/aupress/9781771992732.01

Cover design by Marvin Harder
Interior design by Sergiy Kozakov
Printed and bound in Canada

Library and Archives Canada Cataloguing in Publication
Title: World Bolshevism / Iulii Martov; in a new translation by Mariya
    Melentyeva and Paul Kellogg; with an introduction by Paul Kellogg.
Other titles: Mirovoi bol'shevizm. English.
Names: Martov, L., 1873-1923, author. | Kellogg, Paul, 1955- writer of
    introduction, translator. | Melentyeva, Mariya, translator.
Description: Translation of: Mirovoi bol'shevizm. | Includes bibliographical
    references.
Identifiers: Canadiana (ebook) 20210366478 | Canadiana (print) 20210366427 |
    ISBN 9781771992749 (PDF) | ISBN 9781771992756 (EPUB) |
    ISBN 9781771992732 (paperback)
Subjects: LCSH: Communism—Soviet Union.
Classification: LCC HX313. M3713 2022 | DDC 335.430947—dc23

We acknowledge the financial support of the Government of Canada through
the Canada Book Fund (CBF) for our publishing activities and the assistance
provided by the Government of Alberta through the Alberta Media Fund.

Canada   Alberta
                 Government

Contents

World Bolshevism

III. Decomposition or Conquest of the State?

Photograph of Iulii Martov, taken by police after his arrest in
January 1896.

Introduction

The Lost Voice of Iulii Martov

To students of twentieth-century Russian history, the name Vladimir Il'ich Lenin is a constant, and inevitable, presence. But the name Iulii Osipovich Tsederbaum—better known through the pseudonym "Iulii Martov"—is either entirely absent from view or present only as a mysterious, and often unsavoury, figure. Prior to the revolution of 1917, this would not have been the case. Boris Souvarine would until 1924 be a close collaborator with Lenin. But for Souvarine and others of his generation growing up in France, "Lenin was only an indistinct reference point. Very few people had even heard of him. Trotsky, Martov and Lozovsky were better known."[1] However, Lenin's Bolshevik wing of the Russian Social Democratic Labour Party (Rossiiskaia sotsial-demokraticheskaia rabochaia partiia, or RSDRP) achieved state power, while Martov and the Menshevik wing of the party were suppressed. That suppression was intense, and Martov's writings almost entirely disappeared from view—a remarkable feat given that Martov was a very prolific author.

Like Lenin, a lifelong political journalist, Martov wrote literally hundreds of articles. In addition, his biographer, Israel Getzler, lists fully thirty-six "books and pamphlets" authored by Martov.[2] This voluminous output notwithstanding, it was not until 2000 that an edition of some of his key writings (including sections I and II of *World*

I

Bolshevism) was published in Russia. As its editors noted, "most of these works are reprinted in Russia for the first time, since for many decades it was extremely dangerous even to mention the author's name."[3] Martov's works are almost as scarce in English translation. In 1938, *The State and the Socialist Revolution*—a pamphlet containing sections II and III of *World Bolshevism* in the translation of Herman Jerson—appeared in New York but was never widely circulated, and otherwise readers have been limited to a few excerpts in anthologies and the selections available on the Marxists Internet Archive.[4]

By contrast, as a spinoff from the long-running state-sponsored cult of Lenin (which came to an end only with the collapse of the Soviet Union), we are inundated with material from Lenin—in Russian, English, and many other languages. According to the *Great Soviet Encyclopedia*, "465,714,000 copies of works by Lenin were published in the USSR from 1918 to 1974." This included "355,479,000 copies published in Russian, 70,860,000 in 62 other national languages of the USSR, and 33,975,000 in 39 foreign languages."[5] This is not merely an artifact of the Cold War era. According to UNESCO's Index Translationum, in the first decade of the twenty-first century, Lenin ranked seventh on the list of the world's most translated authors, trailing William Shakespeare and Agatha Christie but ahead of Charles Dickens and Mark Twain.[6]

This absenting of Martov and highlighting of Lenin distorts our view of history. In his era, Martov was without question one of the most important intellectuals and leaders of the Russian Left, including its principal organization, the RSDRP. His contemporary, Alexander Potresov, was not alone in his view that Martov, even when very young, "was essentially predestined to become the center of the party, its truly beloved representative."[7] In my own study of the politics of Martov's era, *"Truth Behind Bars,"* I drew on many of Martov's key writings. Yet on the whole, Martov's works are far less well-known than those of many other writers of the period. As we will see, his name has come to be associated not only with the "reformism" allegedly characteristic of the Mensheviks but also with "social patriotism" (an archaic phrase that I examine in more detail below)—in a manner that often fails to differentiate the anti-war section of the Mensheviks, to which Martov belonged, from the section that came out in support of the war in 1914. Martov was, in fact, a lifelong internationalist, and during the "Great War" he organized the tendency known as "Menshevik-Internationalist" (which we might render in contemporary discourse as "anti-war Menshevik") precisely because he was a passionate opponent of the slaughter. His anti-war and internationalist credentials are absolutely impeccable.

Hence the title for this introduction. The phrase "Martov's voice" references both the prolific political voice—writings and speeches—of this scholar-activist, and his physical voice, virtually mute in the last months of his life as he struggled with what was to be a fatal disease, in the literature variously called tuberculosis or cancer of either the throat or larynx. This disease ultimately cut short his life at the age of forty-nine. We will, of course, never recover Martov's physical voice. But we can hear an echo of his political voice by making available portions of his vast intellectual output, writings that had a wide audience during his lifetime but that have been buried, distorted, and forgotten in the decades since.

Analytically, what has been lost with the silencing of Martov's voice is the framework he and his co-thinkers constructed for understanding the class dynamics of the Russian Revolution, a framework developed in *World Bolshevism* and summarized by Martov's colleague Raphael Abramovitch in *The Soviet Revolution, 1917–1939*.[8] Martov and Abramovitch were historical materialists ("Marxists") trained in the classical tradition of nineteenth-century European social democracy. As such, they saw class struggle as the central aspect of historical development. However, they argued that the traditional categories of class analysis—bourgeoisie, petite bourgeoisie, proletariat, lumpen-proletariat, and so on—were inadequate and misleading when applied schematically to the revolutionary wave that swept Russia and much of Europe after the terrible slaughter of World War I. They argued that a "temporary new class" of peasants and workers in uniform—and, in Russia, this meant overwhelmingly *peasants* in uniform—was the pivotal actor in this revolutionary wave. This temporary new class *was* revolutionary, grimly committed to sweeping all before it in an angry determination to leave the killing fields, return home, and seize control of farm and factory. But this temporary new class was revolutionary in a very particular way. The awful experience of nearly four years in the trenches imbued this temporary new class with a habit of solving political disputes through force of arms. In addition, these peasants and workers in uniform had lost faith in their "democratic socialist" party leaders, who had urged them into the hell of the trenches to kill and maim workers and farmers from other countries. Combined, this created an environment in which democracy—itself a fledgling presence on the Russian political landscape—was seen as contingent rather than essential, in which terror was an acceptable tactic, and in which the "old" traditions of politics and organization were held in contempt. Lenin and the Bolsheviks were able to ride this revolutionary wave to power. But in uncritically adopting a contempt for democracy and the habit of settling disputes with violence, they simultaneously laid the seeds for a reversion to an earlier "utopian" or "Jacobin" form of socialism, and ultimately for the creation of a bureaucratic state based on violence and the suppression of democratic freedoms.[9]

From Tsar to Gulag

The silencing of Martov's voice began under the tsar. In January 1896, at the age of twenty-two, he was arrested for anti-tsarist organizing. Six months later, he began a three-year exile in the subarctic Siberian colony of Turukhansk, a "little decaying town at the end of nowhere," according to Getzler, where "the tuberculosis of the throat which plagued and shortened his life seems to have been contracted."[10]

The silencing of Martov's voice continued in the context of the Civil War period after the 1917 revolution. Martov wrote the twelve chapters of *World Bolshevism* in 1919. The first nine chapters were serialized that same year in several issues of the Menshevik-affiliated journal *Mysl'* (Thought), published out of the eastern Ukrainian city of Kharkiv (or Kharkov, in the Russian spelling). However, at the end of June, General Denikin's so-called Volunteer Army (better understood as a counter-revolutionary "White" army) conquered and occupied the city, ending all left publishing initiatives.[11] Of the remaining three chapters, the Russian text of one (chapter 10) was published in 1921 in *Sotsialisticheskii vestnik* (Socialist courier), the Menshevik journal-in-exile based in Berlin, but the entire work became available only in 1923, in a Russian-language edition also published in Berlin.

But the silencing of Martov's voice was also the result of actions by the revolutionary "Red" state of the Bolsheviks. Martov's wing of the RSDRP—the Menshevik-Internationalists—had much in common with the Bolsheviks, in particular a fierce opposition to the Great War. Almost simultaneously with what was to go down in history as the October Revolution of 1917, Martov's internationalist, anti-war wing wrested full control of the Mensheviks from pro-war socialists and from that point on found themselves caught between the counter-revolutionary Right and the Bolshevik state. Martov and the Mensheviks, under his leadership, opposed those who took up arms against the Bolshevik state as playing into the hands of the counter-revolution while simultaneously opposing the Bolshevik drift into single-party rule. Matters of principle were at stake. The two parties differed on the related questions of democracy and terror. For the Bolsheviks, support for the first and resort to the latter were tactical, contingent questions. For Martov, support for democracy and opposition to terror were matters of principle. Martov and the Mensheviks were thus awkwardly positioned, in Getzler's words, as a "harassed, semi-loyal, semi-irreconcilable opposition" to the new Bolshevik-run state.[12] This led to years of confrontation between the two left groups.

These complex political positions are reflected in the terminology deployed to analyze the events of the period. From the 1920s on, according to an important and detailed 2012 linguistic analysis, the phrase *October revoliutsiia* (October Revolution) became "the only official designation for the event that resulted in the Bolsheviks seizing power."[13] However, in 1917, "the phrase *October perevorot* . . . was used as the official designation . . . along with the phrases *October revoliutsiia* and *October vosstanie*."[14] Importantly, this was the practice of the Bolshevik editors of *Pravda* in 1917, for whom "the words *revoliutsiia* [revolution], *vosstanie* [uprising] and *perevorot* [overturn] were used as quasi-synonyms to refer to the same events," including both the February and October Revolutions.[15] Martov and his co-thinkers held on to the word *perevorot* as their term of choice, a practice highlighted by Leopold Haimson. A quick contemporary translation of *perevorot* might be "coup," or when applied to the events of 1917, "October Revolution"[16] Haimson avoids both and instead uses the English word "overturn."[17] To translate *Oktiabr'skii perevorot* as "October Coup" would imply a completely negative attitude toward the event. To translate it as "October Revolution" would align Martov too closely with the Bolshevik view, with which he had many very serious differences. *Oktiabr'skii perevorot* (the October overturn) aligns most closely with Martov's approach, recognizing as it does the reality of an event of immense importance without any implied reverence for the resulting regime.

The criticisms levelled by Martov against the regime that emerged from the October overturn were pointed, and they were rooted above all in a defence of what he saw as socialist principle. In the conclusion to *"Truth Behind Bars,"* I documented Martov's trenchant criticism of the Bolsheviks' resort to summary executions as a matter of state policy. Seven months after the October overturn, he wrote:

> In every town, in every district, various "Extraordinary Commissions" and "Military-Revolutionary Committees" have ordered the execution of hundreds and hundreds of people.[18] . . . We Social Democrats are opposed to all terror, both from above and from below. Therefore, we are also against the death penalty—this extreme means of terror, of intimidation, to which all rulers resort when they have lost the trust of the people. The struggle against the death penalty was inscribed on the banners of all those who struggled for the freedom and happiness of the Russian people, all those who struggled for socialism.[19]

These attacks on basic freedoms had begun much earlier. Immediately after the Bolshevik victory, liberal newspapers were forcibly suppressed. The revolution's great chronicler, Nikolai Sukhanov, writes that "on the very next day following the victorious uprising the residents of Petersburg found several of the capital's newspapers missing."

> The Military Revolutionary Committee had shut them down—for harassing the Soviets and similar crimes. . . . In the morning, sailors were sent to the distribution centres of *Rech* [Speech] and *Sovremennoe slovo* [Contemporary word]. All available issues were confiscated, taken out into the street in an enormous mass, and immediately set on fire. The never-before-seen *auto-da-fé* attracted a large audience.[20]

The repression of the press was by no means restricted to these liberal publications. Martov's party, just weeks after the October overturn, issued a statement saying that,

> the central organ of our party, the *Workers' Gazette*, has been forcibly shut down, along with other papers, by the War Revolutionary Committee. . . . After our new central organ, *The Ray*, started to appear, the printing works were seized by sailors and Red Guards. . . . These men, whose power is based on bayonets, are determined to prolong their dictatorship and for that purpose are destroying all freedoms including those of the press and assembly, the right to form trade unions and to strike.[21]

In spite of these pressures, Martov and his supporters found ways to reopen their newspapers, which continued to function more or less freely for a few more months. But in June 1918, the Bolsheviks expelled Martov and five other Mensheviks, along with members of the Party of Social Revolutionaries, from their positions in the All-Russian Central Executive Committee (Vserossiiskii Tsentral'nyi Ispolnitel'nyi Komitet, or VTsIK), the leading legislative body of the new state) and again closed down their newspapers.[22] Getzler says this repression "drove them underground, just on the eve of the elections to the Fifth Congress of Soviets in which the Mensheviks were expected to make significant gains. . . . And for the next two years the Bolsheviks were to keep them, somewhat as the tsar had done, in an uncertain state of semi-legal opposition."[23] Nonetheless, organizing continued. An Assembly of Factory and Plant Authorized Representatives convened in July 1918 and elected Raphael Abramovitch as chair. It was quickly dispersed, however, its delegates arrested and, as Abramovitch writes in his first-hand account, "accused of plotting against the Soviet government and threatened with the death penalty." The threat of execution was real, and in September some of Abramovitch's friends managed to obtain permission for his wife to visit him in the prison to say goodbye. In the end, though, his execution was cancelled.[24]

The Mensheviks' semi-legality lasted until the spring of 1920. On 21 May 1920, between 3,000 and 6,000 people attended a meeting hosted by the Moscow printers' union, whose leading bodies at that time still included many Mensheviks. The occasion was a visit from a British Labour Party delegation, on tour to investigate the situation in Soviet Russia. Menshevik leader Fedor Dan shared the platform with many other left leaders, including several Bolsheviks. Toward the end of the meeting an individual described by David Dallin as "a man with a long beard" climbed up onto the platform, where he sought and was granted permission to speak on behalf of the Party of Social Revolutionaries. As he spoke, people came to realize that the long beard was a disguise concealing Victor Chernov, famous leader of the Social Revolutionaries and a man on the run from the Bolshevik state. Dan's eyewitness account is riveting:

> When the speaker had finished, the Bolsheviks began to shout, "What is the name? Let him tell his name!" Chernov stepped forward and identified himself. The result was not what the Bolsheviks had expected. To their bloodhound zeal, to their cries, "Arrest him!" the audience responded with a loud ovation for the quarry, which made the Bolsheviks lose their heads. In the confusion, Chernov disappeared as unnoticeably as he had come.[25]

The 21 May 1920 event was, according to Dallin, "the last big oppositional meeting in the history of the revolution."[26] Once the British delegation left the country, the Bolsheviks took measures to prevent any such display of opposition from happening in the future, removing some non-Bolshevik socialists from positions of leadership, arresting others, sending a few into exile.

Martov and Abramovitch were among those who would find their way into the relative safety of exile, where they were able to continue their political activity in the open. Many others, however, were doomed to disappear into the Gulag prison-camp system. That system came into full flower, of course, under Joseph Stalin.[27] But as early as 1925, Abramovitch co-authored a book, widely distributed among members of the workers' movement outside Russia, documenting the mass internment, from 1923 on, of hundreds of non-Bolshevik Russian socialists in the Solovki prison camp.[28] Anne Applebaum explains that Solovki, established on the subarctic Solovetsky archipelago, came to be known in "survivors' folklore" as the "first camp of the Gulag."[29]

Iulii Osipovich Tsederbaum, Scholar-Activist

Operating under conditions of oppression was an experience familiar to Martov and his generation, particularly for those of a Jewish background. Iulii Osipovich Tsederbaum—the man we know as Iulii Martov—was born in November 1873. Throughout his entire life, his experience as a Jew in the Russian Empire would intersect and combine with his vocation as a socialist organizer—even though Martov was himself extremely secular and only learned Yiddish, the language of the Jewish-Russian proletariat, for political reasons as a young adult. The repression he experienced at the hands of the tsarist state provided him with a profound education in both the struggle of workers against exploitation and the struggle of Russia's Jewish citizens against racism and prejudice—what today we might call an education in "intersectional" politics.[30]

As a teenage student in St. Petersburg, Martov, along with many of his generation, became an anti-tsarist political activist. In February

1892, the nineteen-year-old Martov was arrested for his political work, and after several months in prison (during which he was able to intensify his reading of key political texts), he was ultimately sentenced to two years of "exile from the two capitals"—a reference to Russia's two principal cities, St. Petersburg and Moscow. As a Jewish citizen, he had to receive special sanction to live in these cities, and for two years this sanction was withdrawn. So, in June 1893, the young Martov (still not yet twenty) travelled from St. Petersburg to Vilno, which at the time was nicknamed the "Jerusalem of Lithuania." Vilno (today, Vilnius) was an important city in what was then referred to as the Pale of Settlement, the only territory in the deeply antisemitic Russian Empire in which most Jews could achieve legal permanent residence. He discovered there a deep intersection between working-class socialism and the issues confronting the city's large Jewish population.

In St. Petersburg, Martov and his comrades had labelled themselves the "Petersburg Emancipation of Labour Group." The name reflected a bit of youthful enthusiasm on the part of the group's members, as at the time there were no workers among them.[31] But once in Vilno, he encountered something quite different—a network of socialists who were organizing with "hundreds of young Jewish workers and artisans." He immediately went to work as an educator (or propagandist), teaching three circles of workers "the elementary political economy, politics, and history which would turn his pupils eventually into conscious Marxists."[32] Getzler says that as a Tsederbaum, Martov "was a third- or fourth-generation product of the *Haskalah*, the Jewish enlightenment movement, which was essentially an attempt to gain Jewish emancipation by way of education."[33] In Vilno, Martov was in many ways picking up the thread of the *Haskalah*, striving for emancipation through socialist education.

However, for Martov and some of his friends, the limits of this approach were soon thrown into stark relief. While hundreds of young workers could be drawn to an approach that relied heavily on Russian-language texts, it was impossible to make any headway "among the ten thousand ordinary workers of Vilno who had no educational ambitions, spoke Yiddish, and knew little Russian."[34] Martov and his comrades decided to make a change: they would henceforth shift from a strictly educational approach to one focussing on agitation around the day-to-day economic and social issues faced by the mass of Jewish workers in Vilno, and, importantly, they resolved to carry out their efforts in the workers' own language—Yiddish. Martov helped to distill the essence of this "Vilno program" in what became a widely read pamphlet, *On Agitation*, the main points of which Martov summarized in a speech delivered to four hundred activists during the city's 1895 May Day celebrations. According to Getzler,

> Though agitation was one of its [the pamphlet's] themes, it also had another. With great significance for the future, it may be regarded as the foundation charter of Bundism: the belief that the specific problems of the Jewish proletariat in the Pale of Settlement required the establishment of a separate Jewish labour movement. . . . There is little doubt that it was Martov alone who first collected these current and general ideas into clear formulas and "hard" policies.[35]

Thus it was that "Martov, the assimilated Jew from Petersburg with hardly a word of Yiddish, came to formulate the ideology and the rationale which in 1897 led to the foundation of the Bund," the General Jewish Labour Bund in Lithuania, Poland, and Russia.

Bund leaders were aware of Martov's role in the formation of their movement. In 1900, they republished his 1895 May Day speech with the title "A Turning-point in the History of the Jewish Workers' Movement."[36] But although a core participant in the political ferment that produced that enormously successful mass party based in the Yiddish-speaking proletariat, Martov soon shifted his focus to the publication of Russian-language material and the creation of an "all-Russian" network of activists. This project would end in disarray in 1903 with a complete fracturing of the Russian Left that would see Martov and Lenin first divided from the Bund and then, ultimately, divided from each other. Over the years, Martov's estrangement from the Bund would be healed—the reconciliation symbolized, for instance, in his close collaboration with Abramovitch, a person who was simultaneously a leader of the Bund (an elected member of its Central Committee for many years) and of the Mensheviks.[37]

The split between Martov and Lenin would prove to be much more intractable. Ironically, it came at the conclusion of an intense unity initiative in which the regular production and distribution of émigré publications were used as activities through which the scattered local sections of the Left could be united. This project is almost universally seen as an initiative of Vladimir Lenin's. In fact, three individuals were behind the unification effort. One of these, Alexander Potresov, says that "at the end of the period of our forced internal exile, we founded what Lenin called our 'Triple Alliance' (Lenin, Martov, and myself), with the aim of creating an illegal literary centre for the movement around the newspaper *Iskra* [Spark] and the journal *Zaria* [Dawn] making of these publications tools for building a truly all-Russian, unified, and organized party."[38]

Lenin most clearly outlined the rationale for this attempt at left unity in a 1901 article published in *Iskra* under the title "Where to Begin?" "The role of a newspaper," wrote Lenin, "is not limited solely to the dissemination of ideas, to political education, and to the involvement of political allies."

> The newspaper is not only a collective propagandist and a collective agitator, it is also a collective organizer. In this latter respect it may be likened to the scaffolding round a building under construction, which marks the contours of the structure and facilitates communication between the individual builders, enabling them to distribute the work and to survey the overall results achieved by their organized labour. With the aid of the newspaper, and in connection to it, a permanent organization will take shape that will engage not only in local activities, but also in regular, general work, which will train its members to closely monitor political events, assess their significance and their influence on various strata of the population, and develop effective means for the revolutionary party to influence those events. Just the technical tasks of regularly supplying the newspaper with material and promoting its regular distribution will make

it necessary to create a network of local agents of a united party,
agents who are in active relationship with each other, who know the
general state of affairs, the varied functions of All-Russian work,
and who try their hand at organizing various revolutionary actions.
This network of agents will be the backbone of precisely the kind of
organization we need.[39]

In an almost classically Leninist manner, Martov played the role
of just such an "agent" throughout his life—a journalist, scholar, and
organizer whose work facilitated the construction of a political current. His role in Lenin's "all-Russian" unity project was foundational.
From 1900 until 1903, he was, together with Potresov and Lenin, a
core member of the "Triple Alliance" as they worked together to shape
Iskra and *Zaria*, the poles around which the party was to be recon-
structed. In this organizing work, according to P. Iu. Savel'ev and S. V.
Tiutiukin, "Martov was simply irreplaceable." When it came to work
on *Iskra*, "Lenin acknowledged" that "he and Martov performed all
editorial and technical functions for every issue." Martov was "a first-rate
socio-political commentator, one of those who defined the paper's persona. Forty-nine of Martov's pieces were published in *Iskra* from 1900
through 1903, including thirteen lead articles, while Lenin published
thirty-two articles, including sixteen leaders."[40] The subsequent split
with Lenin would not end this aspect of Martov's activism; indeed, he
continued in this role as a journalist/scholar/organizer until his death.

However, the famously acrimonious 1903 Second Congress of the
RSDRP, as we have seen, permanently shattered the Triple Alliance,
dividing Lenin from Martov and Potresov and, for a time, dividing
Martov and his supporters from the Bund. How did the *Iskra/Zaria*
quest for left unity result in its opposite—the most extreme disunity?

The split with the Bund can be relatively easily understood. The
Russian socialists would not countenance recognizing the Bund as an
autonomous section within the RSDRP, a section with sole responsibility for the Jewish, Yiddish-speaking proletariat. The Bund—which
was a genuine mass party within the Pale of Settlement—saw no
reason to relinquish this autonomy to the much smaller, more rigid

and doctrinaire sections of the party outside the Pale. Their autonomy denied, the Bund delegates left the congress. However, the split between Lenin and Martov is much less easy to understand. The relatively circumscribed nature of the differences between the two men—a subtle disagreement over the party's membership criteria and the composition of the *Iskra* editorial board—was completely out of proportion to the extreme emotions on full display in what Getzler described as "that stormy session in which Lenin and his twenty 'hards' purged the editorial board."[41] Brian Pearce says that there was "an atmosphere of extreme tension" at that session. One delegate "had to be restrained from beating up another delegate."[42] Pearce cites the testimony of Nadezhda Krupskaya:

> The struggle became exceedingly acute during the elections. A couple of scenes just before the voting remain in my memory. Axelrod was reproaching Bauman ("Sorokin") for what seemed to him to be a lack of moral sense, and recalled some unpleasant gossip from exile days. Bauman remained silent, and tears came to his eyes.
> Another scene I remember. Deutsch was angrily reprimanding "Glebov" (Noskov) about something. The latter raised his head, and with gleaming eyes said bitterly: "You just keep your mouth shut, you old dodderer!"[43]

At that stormy session, this same Nikolai Bauman, whom Getzler calls "one of Lenin's best-trusted men," was among those who heckled Martov while he was speaking.[44] Bauman's name will reappear in the course of this narrative.

Tony Cliff articulates what is probably the hegemonic understanding of this unexpected and difficult-to-explain division—a premonition of necessary, inevitable divisions to come: namely, the split between Lenin's "revolutionary" Bolsheviks and Martov's "reformist" Mensheviks.[45] Lars Lih invites us to trouble this standard interpretation, arguing that "the somewhat frustrating debate of 1903–4 was not over the profound issues many people have wanted to read into it. All the same, neither was it a trivial squabble. We can best call it a characteristic split over empirical questions."[46]

In *"Truth Behind Bars"* I point out that, in the moment, key individuals from what came to be called the "Menshevik" side of the division developed a third position, articulating a socialist politics explicitly based on the concept of self-activity. According to Leopold Haimson, *"samoupravlenie, samostoiatel'nost' samodeiatel'nost'* [lit. self-government, autonomy, self-activity] were terms used by the Mensheviks to express the need for the 'active involvement' of workers in public affairs," and these "were developed by the Menshevik editors of *Iskra* following their 1903 split with Lenin."[47] Pavel Axelrod, in an influential article, the first part of which was published in late 1903, the second in early 1904, outlined these ideas at some length, arguing that "the development of class self-awareness and the self-activity of the proletariat is a process of self-development and self-education of the working class," the indispensable foundation for the "process of social-democratic self-development and self-education."[48] The young Leon Trotsky (at the time just twenty-four years old), in his first major work, *Our Political Tasks*, argued that the publication of Axelrod's article marked "the beginning of a new era in our movement."[49] "The basic task," Trotsky argued, "may in general be formulated as consisting of the development of the self-activity of the proletariat."[50]

An in-depth exploration of self-activity and its opposite, substitutionism, is undertaken in *"Truth Behind Bars."* Relevant here is another, fourth aspect to the bitter divide, prominent at the time but largely hidden from history in subsequent decades, one with profoundly *ethical* rather than simply empirical dimensions.

The Ethical Dimension

In the months leading up to the 1903 split, the principal protagonists had become enmeshed in a private and increasingly toxic cauldron of dysfunctional personal relations. Potresov describes the atmosphere among the members of the *Iskra* editorial board as one of "increasingly fierce political struggle" leading to "an extremely unpleasant aggravation" in their common work.[51] Lenin described this time as "three years of 'legalistic wrangling.'"[52] He would also famously pin the blame for this toxicity on what he believed to be the psychological indecisiveness inherent to the intelligentsia—an aspect of his thought covered *in extenso* in *"Truth Behind Bars."* Potresov sees it quite differently, pinning the blame on Lenin, whom he called "a sectarian who had a serious Marxist training behind him, a Marxist sectarian!"[53] Potresov goes on to say that "the atmosphere surrounding Lenin was poisoned from the very outset by the fact that Lenin, in essence, was organically incapable of tolerating opinions that differed from his own, and consequently every editorial dispute tended to degenerate into a conflict accompanied by an acute aggravation of personal relations." Lenin approached these debates deploying "war-like measures," struggling to "gain the upper hand for his views, no matter the cost."[54]

In early 1903, six months before the formal split, these tensions indeed exploded into open warfare. The issue was no longer one of mere personal friction but differences over standards of behaviour inside the party. Potresov's account is grim:

> Half a year before the party congress of 1903, at which the split in the party became a fact, relations between Lenin on the one hand, and Martov, Vera Zasulich and myself on the other—relations which had already become strained—broke down completely. The chance occasion that drew our attention to this Leninist amoralism and knocked the bottom out of the barrel was the resistance Lenin put up—with boundless cynicism—to the investigation into an accusation made by a complainant against one of the agents closest to him. All such accusations, even if they involved the death of a human being, were for Lenin only annoying obstacles standing in the way of his political successes, and as obstacles they were simply to be brushed aside.[55]

Lenin acknowledged the bitterness of this incident, saying that in the heat of debate, his opponents had called him and his ally Plekhanov "fiends and monsters" for defending a man whom Martov, Potresov, and Zasulich "all but 'condemned' ... *politically* for an incident of a purely personal nature."[56] But neither Lenin nor Potresov offer any meaningful details as to the nature of this incident.

To get those details, the best account comes from Lidiia Osipovna Dan (Martov's sister), an account she provided to Leopold Haimson as part of a series of remarkable interviews recorded from exile in New York in the 1960s. Dan was a lifelong socialist, a key activist in the *Iskra* project, and from 1903 until her death in 1963, a committed member of the Menshevik wing of the party. Nikolai Bauman—referred to above as "one of Lenin's best-trusted men"—was someone Dan knew "fairly well," someone she described as being "rather derisive" and "enormously successful [*sic*] among his women comrades." When in exile in Viatka province in the late 1890s, Bauman developed a relationship with another party activist, Claudia (Klavdiia) Prikhodko. After the couple broke up, Prikhodko "took up with" with another party activist, Metrov, who "helped her out, since she was very depressed."[57] Getzler tells a very similar story, although in his account (and those of all others) Claudia Prikhodko remains anonymous.[58]

These intertwined personal relationships became a party issue after Prikhodko discovered she was pregnant. Bauman, who "could draw rather well ... drew a caricature which everyone immediately recognized—Klavdiia as the Virgin Mary with a child in her womb, and a question mark asking who the baby looked liked. In short, it was pretty malicious, on the verge of being indecent. She was apparently very distraught, and committed suicide, hung herself."[59]

Metrov (identified as "M." by Getzler) brought to the *Iskra* editorial board, "as the highest party tribunal," Claudia Prikhodko's fifteen-page suicide note, dated 28 January 1902. In that note, according to Getzler,

> she appealed to the party, "the party of the struggle for freedom, the dignity, and the happiness of man": she complained of the "prevailing indifference" in the party to the "personal morality" of comrades, and expressed the hope that her "undeserved end" might "draw the attention of comrades to the question of the private morals of public figures."[60]

The appeal was unsuccessful. Lenin, to the dismay of Potresov, Martov, and Zasulich, ruled it out of order as a purely personal matter, outside the competence of *Iskra* and detrimental to the interests of the party."[61] Together with the grandee of the movement, G. V. Plekhanov, Lenin outlined the minority "dissenting" position in October 1902: "We find that the case, raised by Comrade Metrov, is a purely personal matter. . . . It cannot and, we firmly believe, *should not* be examined by any revolutionary organization at all. In particular, we, for our part, do not see at the present time absolutely any grounds for instituting actions against N. E. B[auman]."[62] Ultimately, on 17 October 1902, Lenin and Plekhanov accepted a resolution from Martov to shelve the issue. Martov wrote that "in view of the differences revealed in the meeting . . . the editorial board and the administration did not consider it possible to investigate it."[63] How did Lenin and Plekhanov, by all accounts in a clear minority on this issue, get their way over the majority? "*We were in the minority*," Lenin wrote, "but we won by sheer persistence, by threatening to bring everything into the open."[64]

To the extent that this incident has stayed in the historical record, it has done so perversely. Bauman's name is ubiquitous and revered inside Russia. During the turmoil of the 1905 revolution, Bauman was imprisoned for his role leading the Bolshevik organization in Moscow. According to Abraham Ascher, just after his release in October 1905, while leading a demonstration, he was "shot and then beaten to death by a worker sympathetic to the Black Hundreds," a far-right anti-revolutionary group. His funeral procession was the occasion for one of the Bolshevik Party's first mass demonstrations, attracting anywhere from 30,000 to 150,000 people.[65] In subsequent decades, he has had factories, schools, streets, and even an entire district of Moscow named after him.[66] By contrast, Bauman's victim, Claudia Prikhodko, remains almost unknown—in most accounts, anonymous.

Potresov links the months-long personal friction on the editorial board with the sharp disagreement over how to deal with Bauman's sexual misconduct, saying that, together, they provided evidence of Lenin's firm belief that it did not matter *how* something was accomplished, only that the desired result be achieved. Potresov saw this as extraordinary, labelling it with an exclamation mark as "the end justifies the means!" and calling Lenin "the most consistent adherent of this Machiavellian political recipe."[67] Potresov uses the term "amoralism" (*Amoralismus*) to describe such an approach, where in today's language we might instead talk of an "ethical deficit."

Potresov, in many ways, was ahead of his time: he insisted on the inseparability of the "political" and the "personal" at a time when many of his contemporaries maintained a sharp distinction between the two. Indeed, it would take the rise of second-wave feminism later in the century for an explicit and widespread recognition of the fact that the personal *is* political. In its first iterations, the concept was applied specifically to the situation of women. As Barbara Ryan articulated it, "what appeared to be a personal issue was actually a political one that occurred because of unequal gender relations." In the decades since, this insight has been extended to all manifestations of oppression. "Domination of one group over another," continues Ryan, "whatever the guise, leads to the awareness that the personal is, indeed, political."[68] The personal *is* political—or perhaps better, relations within the realm we designate as "personal" often reflect, or are connected to, relations at a societal level, relations we designate as "political." We now understand that everyday bullying and microaggressions are manifestations not only of psychological issues but of systemic oppression as well. The bully, simply put, is socially constructed.[69] This understanding is the necessary foundation for our century's #MeToo movement. A personally abusive and bullying relationship between a man and a woman is not something that we leave them to sort out on their own. These behaviours have public and political dimensions—and consequences. These insights from contemporary movements were developed generations after the early twentieth-century debates inside the Russian Left. But that should not prevent us from using these insights to adjust and focus our own rear-view mirror, helping us to more clearly see the contours of those long-ago events.

The Hamlet Distraction

Martov's organizing work in the years following the 1903 split are far less known than Lenin's. But his efforts were intense and effective—and always framed by his principled anti-war internationalism.

An iconic moment in the reconstruction of an internationalist Left occurred in 1915 with the convening of the anti-war conference in Zimmerwald, Switzerland. Bruno Naarden says that the Russian Axelrod, "the Italian Morgari, the Swiss Grimm and the Dutchman Troelstra were of importance in launching international socialist discussion about the war and in opening up the way to Zimmerwald. Martov performed a comparable role in Paris."[70] Getzler confirms Martov's importance to this project:

> Though the original initiative came from the Italian socialists, it seems to have been Martov who . . . during his visit to Paris in April 1915 . . . appealed to Robert Grimm to replace what was planned as a conference of socialists of neutral countries only, by an international conference of all socialists pledged to peace.[71]

Similarly, with the outbreak of the Great War, Martov played a crucial role as a journalist-scholar-organizer. In France, the newspaper *Golos* (The Voice) "had been founded by unemployed typesetters, who invited Martov to head the publication."[72] Martov declined that onerous role, most likely because of his chronic tuberculosis, a disease that would kill him just a few years later. He did, however, agree to participate in what was to become an extraordinary collective of fellow journalists, scholars, and organizers.[73] According to Savel'ev and Tiutiukin, "Martov immediately emerged as the foremost contributor to that low-circulation internationalist newspaper, small but attention-getting, which came to occupy a conspicuous place in the life not only of the Russian revolutionary intelligentsia but also, perhaps, of the entire international socialist movement."[74] This description might be too modest. *Golos* was the first of three names for a *daily* socialist anti-war paper that was published in Paris from 13 September 1914 until being banned by French authorities after its 26 January 1915 issue—reappearing as *Nashe slovo* (Our word) from 29 January 1915 to 15 September 1916, in turn replaced by *Nachalo* (The Beginning), which continued to March 1917.[75] At one point, Lenin described *Golos* as "the best socialist newspaper in Europe."[76] This newspaper was crucial in the organizing and training of an internationalist anti-war cadre—all of whom were to play key roles in the events of 1917. In its first years, Martov was central to this project.

This Martov—the anti-war journalist-scholar-organizer, the person of strong ethical conviction—is rarely visible in discussions of the Russian Revolution. This is true even in the account of Victor Serge, who, on meeting with Martov in 1920, praised him as someone "whose honesty and brilliance were of the first order" but also described him as "puny, ailing, and limping a little . . . a man of scruple and scholarship, lacking the tough and robust revolutionary will that sweeps obstacles aside."[77]

Serge's masculinist, ableist gaze has no place in serious scholarship. From a very young age, Martov, along with his friends and family, faced obstacles that he had constantly to sweep aside, in the process exhibiting plenty of "tough and robust revolutionary will." In May 1881, at the age of seven, he witnessed his family's response to an anti-Jewish pogrom in Odessa. Getzler, relying on Martov's memoirs, describes the events vividly:

> The father being away in Petersburg, the Tsederbaum household "began to prepare itself for the pogrom"; his uncle rushed in bearing a revolver, while his mother boiled water to pour on the hooligans. Significantly enough she refused the offer of Captain Pereleshin, the chief of police, to post two cossacks for their protection, "convinced as she was, that the cossacks would be the first to take part in the pogrom." . . . Luckily the pogrom had spent itself before it reached their street.[78]

After surviving this pogrom, Martov, while travelling by train back to St. Petersburg, heard from a person Getzler describes as "an Old Jew" the story of another terrible pogrom, this one in Elizavetgrad. In 1922, writing near the end of his life, Martov reflected on the formative nature of these experiences:

> Would I have become what I became had not Russian reality in that memorable night speedily impressed her coarse fingers into the plastic young soul, and under the cover of that burning pity which she stirred up in the childish heart, have planted with care the seeds of saving hatred.[79]

In St. Petersburg, where Martov's family moved in the autumn of 1881, Getzler says that he "had to face the rough-and-ready world of the state gymnasium," and offers the following comment: "Thus it came about that the well-behaved, diligent and rather quiet little boy, who had entered the high school, had turned before the year was over into a fully-fledged rebel, constantly breaking school regulations, daily detained after class, and becoming a sure candidate for expulsion."[80]

As for the limp? When just a baby, he was dropped by a wet nurse, who "kept the incident secret. It was noticed only when he began to walk."[81]

Unfortunately, Serge's dismissive attitude reflects a hegemonic approach to assessments of Martov, one that focusses on aspects of his physicality, and according to which his political contributions are typically subsumed under the headline of psychology rather than politics. Getzler says that Martov's critics claimed that "he was too intellectual (Sukhanov), lacked the will to action and power (Trotsky and Rappoport), had too many scruples (Lunacharsky), and was too doctrinaire (Kuskova, Ryss, and Vishniak)."[82] Leon Trotsky, in a 1919 profile of Martov, predicted that he would "enter the history of the workers' revolution as its leading minus. His thought lacked courage, his insight lacked will. . . . Deprived of the mainspring of a strong will, Martov's thought invariably directed all the strength of its analysis to theoretically justifying the line of least resistance."[83] In 1930, Trotsky deployed the English language's most iconic metaphor for indecision, labelling Martov the "Hamlet of democratic socialism."[84] This approach to Martov's scholarship has remained common practice this century. Ben Lewis calls Martov "politically indecisive".[85] In the same book, without comment or mention of Trotsky as the source, we are offered "Martov: Hamlet of the Russian Revolution" to serve as a caption for a photo of the man.[86] China Miéville, who on the centenary of 1917 published a very helpful contribution to the literature on the Russian Revolution, does weave Martov sympathetically into his story. But when he first introduces Martov, he describes him as "a scrawny figure peering through pince-nez over a thin beard. . . . Weak and bronchial, mercurial, talkative but a hopeless orator, not much better as an organiser, affecting, in these early days, a worker's get-up, Martov is every inch the absent-minded intellectual."[87]

There are at least three serious problems with these glosses on the man's life. First, most of these commentators turn again and again to questions of psychology—specifically, to speculation as to Martov's willpower (or lack thereof). About this we can ask the same question posed regarding speculations concerning Lenin's personality and lifestyle in *"Truth Behind Bars"*: How do we know? While Trotsky, Sukhanov, Lunacharsky, Serge, and the other authorities cited here have credentials as political scholars and political organizers, they have none as psychologists.

Second, what about Martov's many crucial intellectual contributions to the movement, noticed by Miéville and Serge but ignored by most others? We hear that he is "too intellectual," "too doctrinaire," "absent-minded"—but we hear nothing about the rich and varied content of his intellectual output. There is no need to summarize that content again—Martov's many intellectual contributions have been outlined *in extenso* here and in *"Truth Behind Bars."*

Third, labelling Martov as a poor organizer, let alone someone lacking in willpower or courage, simply flies in the face of the evidence. This was a man whose youthful political writings were foundational to the first generation of Bund leaders, whose organizing efforts played a central role in the creation and early operation of *Iskra* and *Zaria*, in the establishment of the RSDRP and the Menshevik-Internationalists, in the building of an anti-war Left in the teeth of imperialist slaughter, and in the development of a robust and vocal, if harassed and hounded, opposition to the degeneration of the Russian Revolution. How can someone who paid for this lifetime of organizing with repeated bouts of repression and exile (where he contracted the tuberculosis that would ultimately kill him) be called a poor organizer or accused of lacking in courage? He overcame the deep antisemitic prejudice characteristic of the Russian Empire (and most of Europe, for that matter) to become a central figure in both Russian revolutions. Martov's life incorporates achievements of intellect and organization matched by very few who call themselves political journalists, scholars, or organizers. A century's worth of flippant dismissals of a key historical figure—as well as being misleading and full of factual errors—are both insulting and unhelpful.

Let us return to Trotsky's 1919 sketch of Martov's life and work, referred to above—an article made widely available, for a time, when published in 1926 in *Politicheskie siluety* (Political profiles), volume 8 of Trotsky's *Sochineniia* (Works). The latter was an important but unfortunately incomplete publishing project brought to an abrupt halt when Trotsky became *persona non grata*—driven from leadership, expelled from the Soviet Union, shunned, and ultimately assassinated.[88] I. M. Pavlov, editor of the truncated *Sochineniia* project, decided to include Trotsky's piece in a section of volume 8 titled "Russian Social-Patriotism." This section contains five articles, the first three of which are devoted to G. V. Plekhanov, one of the founders of Russian Marxism. When, on 4 August 1914, the world's largest and most powerful socialist party, Germany's Social Democratic Party (SPD), voted to provide government funds for the war, it began a stampede by socialists almost everywhere to discard anti-war internationalism in favour of nationalism and support for their own countries' militaries. In Russia, Plekhanov became the embodiment of this "social patriotism"—a phrase used to refer to socialists who supported Russia's war against Germany and tried to justify it as a "defensive" or "just war," their socialist ideas inevitably sinking under what Trotsky calls "the weight of national-patriotic ideology."[89] The fifth article is devoted to Grigorii Aleksinskii, a one-time Bolshevik who in 1914 emerged as what

Pavlov describes as "one of the most rabid Russian social-chauvinists."[90] Toward both men, Trotsky deploys his not inconsiderable skills as a polemicist. Both "Negodiai" (The Scoundrel), which was directed at Aleksinskii, and "Ostav'te nas v pokoe" (Leave us alone), directed at Plekhanov, ooze with the contempt Trotsky felt for social patriotism and the betrayal it represented to the anti-war movement.[91]

Sandwiched between his deconstruction of Plekhanov and Aleksinskii is the equally sarcastic and dismissive piece on Martov.[92] This is an extraordinary and unjustifiable editorial choice. In no way can Martov—against the world war from the beginning, one of the principal animators of the Zimmerwald anti-war movement, and a key organizer of *Golos* in 1914, which was to become the chief Russian-language anti-war newspaper—be categorized as a "Russian social patriot." The editorial decision to place in this category Trotsky's article on Martov makes no sense—unless, of course, the object of the exercise is to shovel mud onto Martov's reputation by placing him in the same category as Plekhanov and Aleksinskii. Trotsky, who knew very well Martov's anti-war credentials, evidently did not object to this editorial shaming of Martov; indeed, he directed toward the editor Pavlov "and his colleagues" his "heartfelt gratitude for the work done on this book."[93] The injustice to Martov's reputation has, unfortunately, been perpetuated in English translation. In 1972, when the first section of volume 8 of Trotsky's *Sochineniia* was translated and published, the article on Martov remained in the "Russian Social-Patriotism" section, an error in judgment that was replicated once again when the 1972 translation was made available online by the Marxists Internet Archive.[94]

Behind by a Century

Martov struggled with repression and illness till the very end of his life. The debilitating effects of the disease he contracted as a result of tsarist repression were on full display on 15 October 1920. Martov had been invited to a congress of the Independent Social Democratic Party (Unabhängige Sozialdemokratische Partei Deutschlands, or USPD) in Halle, Germany, to debate Bolshevik leader Grigory Zinoviev, who was urging the USPD to join forces with the Bolsheviks in the new Communist International, something Martov believed would doom the Left in Germany to replicating the mistaken policies being carried out in Russia. The difficulty of Martov's situation cannot be overstated. The USPD was a mass party in 1920, with something approaching 800,000 members and a lively press that "included over 50 daily papers,"[95] but it was bitterly divided over its attitude to the Bolshevik state. Martov's speech was delivered before 392 mandated delegates sitting in a hall "divided in two sections," according to his opponent Zinoviev, "as if a knife has cut them sharply in two," along with "many observers . . . crammed into the gallery at the back of the hall."[96] He had to follow on the heels of Zinoviev, who spoke for over four hours![97] Lars T. Lih, in introducing his translation of Martov's speech, says that Martov that day was "in poor voice and his speech was read aloud for him."[98] But "poor voice" completely minimizes the situation. Martov was in "poor voice" because of the tuberculosis that was shortly to prove fatal.[99] He wrote the speech out in longhand. It was then read to the audience in German by Aleksandr Nikolaevich Shtein (Rubinshtein), who had "difficulty reading Martov's handwriting."[100] In spite of these extraordinary obstacles, Savel'ev and Tiutiukin write that the speech "made a powerful impression on the delegates and palpably undercut the effect of the rather emphatic address delivered by Zinoviev."[101]

It became clear after the Halle congress that Martov was, in Getzler's words, "mortally ill." In exile in Germany, he was confined to a health-care facility for four months in 1921, and then again from November 1922 until his death in April 1923.[102] But, until the end, he continued his role as one of his generation's leading political figures. As a "member of the Executive of the 'Vienna International' the International Union of Socialist Parties," writes Getzler, Martov "maintained close connections with the socialist centre parties of Europe."[103] He was also central to the founding, in Berlin, of the biweekly Russian-language publication *Sotsialisticheskii vestnik* (Socialist courier), which, in the estimation of Savel'ev and Tiutiukin, "printed nothing more vivid and profound from 1921 to early 1923 than Martov's own eighty-plus articles."[104] Though

Martov would only be present for two years of the publication's existence, *Vestnik*, which André Liebich describes as "a unique and respected journal of Soviet developments and socialist theory," would continue for over forty years.[105]

Raphael Abramovitch wrote eloquently about his friend and mentor in a 1959 article whose title—including as it did the phrase "World Menshevism"—was a riff on Martov's own *World Bolshevism*, written forty years earlier. Abramovitch noted that the mocking and deconstruction of Martov, summarized here, was a well-established practice as early as 1918. What Abramovitch labelled the "pro-Bolshevik gutter press" would portray Martov "in a somewhat ridiculous and caricatured form," often mocking his physical attributes, including his voice made hoarse by tuberculosis. In reports on meetings at which Martov and Lenin were both present, the two would regularly be painted with quite opposite colours. In those reports,

> Martov always went up to the podium, limping, his jacket pockets stuffed with bundles and bundles of newspapers, documents and manuscripts. He would turn to Lenin and wheeze something not quite intelligible. Lenin would look away, so as not to meet the eyes of his former closest friend. The contrast between the physical weakness of the leader of the anti-Bolshevik socialists and the spectacle of the iron cohort of Bolsheviks—sitting or standing on the podium like knights clad in "leather armour" (an expression that often appeared in the afore-mentioned press)—would symbolize the weakness and helplessness of the defeated opposition and the power and dynamism of victorious Bolshevism.

But if this was the image created by what Abramovitch described as the "jaundiced journalism of Bolshevism," a very different impression was given by those willing to listen to Martov during his many speeches. "In 1918 and 1919 Martov invariably spoke during the stormy sessions of the Congress of Soviets, the All-Russian Central Executive Committee, and at even larger meetings."

His face, though already emaciated, still inspired with its wonderful eyes, chiselled nose, and high forehead. He emanated some kind of attractive force, which atoned for his physical limitations, and testified to an elevated flight of thought and great spiritual honesty and warmth. There was no trace of demagoguery, no pursuit of cheap effects, nor any attempt to hide behind fake phrases and paradoxes. He spoke simply, clearly, with a tremendous persuasiveness, which made him trusted.[106]

We are in fact, "behind by a century."[107] We need to foreground *this* Martov and rescue his reputation from decades of calumny. Taking seriously Martov as a person will help remove the obstacles to taking seriously the framework he advanced for understanding the events of 1917. Martov, in an offhand way, says in *World Bolshevism* that the central role of a temporary new class, the peasants-in-uniform, had been "in its time, adequately analyzed."[108] Perhaps that was true for the milieu of embattled dissidents in which he was immersed. For analysts in the twenty-first century, however, it is no longer true. Some emphasize the minimal role of workers and the central role of the armed forces in the October overturn. But very few view the armed forces through the lens of historical materialism, seeing this in class terms—the formation, through war, of a temporary new class. Many concur that the events of October should not be seen as a "great, socialist" revolution. But very few do so with a sense of loss—the lost opportunity of an alternative to capitalism opened up by the events of February and March 1917. As a reflection of this, few insist on the use of the descriptor *perevorot* (overturn) as an alternative to the binary of "revolution" or "coup."

One of the last to weave these themes together was another of the Mensheviks in exile, Grigorii Aronson. His last book, published in 1966, touches on all of the major points mentioned above. "It is very important to note," he writes "that, in the factories and plants of Petrograd, work was in full swing on 25 October," the point on the old calendar when the Bolsheviks took power—an event that Aronson agrees is best described as an "overturn." As to the role of the proletarian Red Guards, he says this "turned out to be a bluff. Suffice it to mention that at the Putilov factory," by most accounts the most important Bolshevik-influenced workplace, "there turned out to be only 80 Red Guards available for Bolshevik operations, not the mythical 1,500."[109] In the one chapter from his book that has achieved a wider circulation, he embeds this observation in an analysis completely in step with Martov's:

> It should not be forgotten that the broad strata of the Russian workers—especially new workers, created by the demands of the war—were intimately connected to the peasantry: and it was the peasantry in the form of soldiers, peasant sons dressed in grey overcoats, that was the main social base of Bolshevism during October and was the main factor in the movement.[110]

However, this kind of emphasis is the exception rather than the rule. Martov died before his fiftieth birthday. Intellectuals like Aronson and Abramovitch developed and deepened his insights, but by the end of the 1960s, both had also passed away, along with most of the other Mensheviks in exile. While these intellectuals had seen their ideas circulate widely within the Yiddish- and Russian-speaking Soviet diaspora, with their passing and the decline of the diaspora as a distinct entity within Western society, their ideas, too, faded into the background. A century on, Martov's thesis—his description of the pivotal role played by the temporary new class of peasants-in-uniform—has been pushed into the background, along with Martov himself. This aspect of the revolution has been inadequately analyzed and its chief theorist too little appreciated. Making available again this 1919 monograph allows us—a century after the fact—to listen again to this important framework and to hear at least an echo of Martov's voice.

World
Bolshevism

A Note on the Translation

Iulii Martov composed the monograph *World Bolshevism* (*Mirovoi bol'shevizm*) in 1919. Yet only nine of its twelve chapters were published that year. It was only in 1923, in the months after his death, that the Russian text appeared in its entirety in one volume—a Russian-language edition prepared by Fedor Dan and published in Berlin by Martov's co-thinkers in exile, complete with an appendix, an essay originally published in Moscow in 1918. Only in 2000 were portions of the book published within Russia. In English translation, Martov's text has had very limited circulation. In 1938, sections II and III (chapters 6 to 12) and the appendix essay were translated by Herman Jerson and published in New York as a pamphlet titled *The State and the Socialist Revolution* (with an updated and annotated version published decades later by the British journal *What Next?*). But the 1938 translation omitted the five chapters in section I. At last, in 2008, an English-language translation of that first section, "The Roots of World Bolshevism," was made available on the Marxists Internet Archive, although the translator is not identified.

In this edition, Martov's book is for the first time presented in its entirety in English-language translation—all twelve chapters and the appendix as published in Russian in 1923. Throughout, Mariya Melentyeva and I, while retaining some elements from earlier translations, have adopted a "minimalist" approach, sticking as closely as possible to the structure and style of Martov's original, including preserving all his many points of emphasis.

The many quotations in the text—some in Russian, which Mariya Melentyeva and myself worked on together, others in English, French, and German, for which I took sole responsibility—had to be brought into line with the contemporary literature, avoiding wherever possible "twice-removed" translations. For instance, Martov uses many French-language sources in his treatment of the Paris Commune and quotes extensively from several non-Russian authors, including Karl Marx and Karl Kautsky. He either used the existing Russian translations of those texts or provided his own translation, in both cases creating a Russian-language version at "one remove" from the original. If we were simply to take his Russian translation and translate it directly from Russian to English, we would be at "two removes" from the original. So, where possible, we have used standard English translations of the texts concerned. Where none could be found, we have translated directly from the original—in the case of the section on the Paris Commune, for example, from the French original to English. In certain cases, even where standard English translations exist, we have either amended those translations to some extent, where some clarification or improvement seemed necessary, or have chosen not to use them in favour of a fresh translation. On occasion, small errors were discovered in the original and these have either been "silently" corrected or, if necessary, the corrections indicated in the endnotes. On other occasions, Martov's Russian-language excerpts differed to a lesser or greater extent from contemporaneous sources. The English translations have been amended to account for these factors, and again those amendments are indicated in the endnotes.

When Martov is quoting from Russian-language sources, these quotations have been checked against the standard sources available to a contemporary audience. For Lenin's *Collected Works*, this meant comparing the English-language versions in the readily available fourth edition, *Lenin: Collected Works* (*LCW*), against the Russian-language version in the standard fifth edition, *Polnoe sobranie sochinenii* (Complete collected works) (*PSS*), amending and retranslating where necessary. Again, on occasion, Martov's Russian-language version differed to a lesser or greater extent from the sources we were using, and this is so indicated in the endnotes. On two occasions, where it was impossible to track down the originals from which Martov was quoting, there was no choice but to translate directly from Martov's version, and to leave a note indicating "translated directly from Martov."

In addition to endnotes indicating the works cited, there are also citations that Martov himself provided, along with notes added by the editor of the 1923 edition, Martov's brother-in-law Fedor Dan (whose life partner was Martov's sister, Lidiia). Within these notes a concluding "—*Martov*" or "—*Dan*" will clearly indicate who is responsible for the material presented. All others are my responsibility. Most of these are annotations which I thought necessary to help a twenty-first century reader navigate the many historical, biographical, and cultural allusions used by Martov.

As in *"Truth Behind Bars,"* transliteration of Russian names and terms follows the system used by the American Library Association (ALA) and the Library of Congress (LC), although without recourse to diacritics—except where a name has acquired a standard English spelling, such as Abramovitch, Kerensky, Krupskaya, Lunacharsky, Trotsky and Zinoviev. For Martov's first name, we have two standards, "Julius" and "Iulii." As in *"Truth Behind Bars,"* the text uses the latter, a transliteration that offers a reasonable clue in English as to the correct pronunciation, as well as being as true as possible to the Cyrillic alphabet. Mariya Melentyeva pointed out to me that for authors of Martov's generation, German was a much more important second language than English, and it was quite reasonable to use "Julius Martow" as the transliteration of Martov's name in German, encouraging English-language translators to use "Julius Martov." But this leads to a distinct mispronunciation of his first name, the German *j* being pronounced like the English *y*.

Martov was a European intellectual deeply immersed in the mores and culture of his day. This meant that, like many of his peers, he took for granted a framework whereby some countries were deemed "advanced" and others "backward." Where possible, we have made translation choices that preserve the original meaning but are less discordant to a contemporary ear. There remain, however, several paragraphs, involving brief comparative descriptions of the place within the world system of various nations, that reflect the Eurocentrism typical of Martov's generation of European intellectuals.

Until February 1918, Russia used the Julian calendar, whose dates were thirteen days behind the Gregorian. On a handful of occasions, I will provide both dates, putting the Julian first, followed by the Gregorian in parentheses.

Mariya Melentyeva was indispensable in helping to translate the text from Russian to English. Megan Hall, director of Athabasca University Press, skillfully helped navigate the copy editing and production process. The Russian-language copy editing of Elizabeth Adams from World Communications, and the copy-editing of the entire text by Ryan Perks led to a much-improved final product. Many thanks to Adrian Mather for preparing a professional and comprehensive index.

It was an unexpected pleasure to read this manuscript, discovered while researching *"Truth Behind Bars."* What began as an exercise in ensuring the accuracy of English translations of excerpts from the text became a labour of love as I realized the importance of the document Martov had penned, in the very midst of the great upheavals of his era. One hundred years is long enough for this document to be out of circulation.

Mackenzie Paul Kellogg
Toronto, November 2021

Foreword to the 1923 Russian-language Edition

The book *World Bolshevism* was left unfinished by the late Iulii Osipovich Martov. A life disrupted by exile, constant overwork, serious illness, and the suppression of the independent press in Russia—including the social-democratic Kharkiv journal *Mysl'* (Thought), for which these essays were originally intended—deprived the great publicist of the opportunity to finish the major work he had begun.

But the twelve chapters that Martov managed to write in 1919 are of absolutely exceptional interest. These chapters offer the deepest and most penetrating analysis of all that has been written concerning the social, ideological, and psychological origins of Bolshevism as a world phenomenon and about its ideology and the relation of this ideology to Marxism. Martov wields a sharp scalpel of historical analysis to reveal the spiritual connection of the Bolshevik proletarian movement to the movements of the 1871 commune era, to English Chartism, and even further in history to the movement of the Parisian "common poor" during the Great French Revolution. At the same time, his analysis is materialist and framed by the conditions of the class struggle. He thus explains the ideological relationship of movements separated from each other by more than a century of time. And finally, with his usual skill, Martov restores the actual theoretical views of Marx and Engels concerning the essence of the "dictatorship of the proletariat" and the relationship of this dictatorship to the state.

The array of profound matters touched on by Martov in this work are by no means of only academic significance. They are of the most burning practical interest for the political education of all who are convinced that above everything else, all politics should be based on an exhaustive understanding of the social and political phenomena at play. These phenomena will probably continue to play a significant role for a long time in the turbulent postwar events that yesterday shook eastern Europe, today shake the very heart of Europe, and tomorrow might well shake the whole world.

All twelve chapters offered here were written in the first half of 1919, in Moscow. Of these, chapters 1 to 9 were published in nos. 10, 12, 13, and 15 of the Kharkiv journal *Mysl'* (Thought) (April–July 1919). Chapter 10 appeared in no. 11 (8 July 1921) and no. 15 (1 September 1921) of *Sotsialisticheskii vestnik* (Socialist courier), published in Berlin. Somewhat abridged versions of chapters 1 to 5 were also printed in German translation in nos. 46, 48, and 49 (November–December 1920) of the journal *Der Sozialist* (The Socialist), published in Berlin under the editorship of R[udolf] Breitscheid. Chapters 11 and 12 have never before been published.

We gathered material for the book from Martov's papers, which were in great disarray. They consisted of: (1) clippings from the journal *Mysl'* (Thought); (2) typewritten sheets; and (3) scattered handwritten notes. There were some corrections and additions in Martov's handwriting on the journal clippings and typewritten sheets. He also provided titles for sections II and III and chapters 6 to 10 and 12— some of these titles (for section II and for chapters 6 to 9) were written in German, clearly in order to assist with the task of publishing them in German. All amendments and additions are included in the text of this version. We have restored those editorial deletions that were clearly only made for the purposes of the German edition.

The editor's task was very modest. It consisted, mainly, in the selection and verification of material. Further, the editor is responsible for the titles of section I and all five of that section's chapters, as well as the title of chapter II in section III. Finally, I felt it necessary to add—to a very limited extent—a number of endnotes throughout the text.

While reading this work, one should not lose sight of the fact that all of it was written in 1919, and only minor additions were made later. The lived experiences that Martov uses to illustrate his thoughts date to this period, and we felt it was necessary to add the occasional endnote for clarification.

In the appendix we reprint an article by Martov, "Marx and the Problem of the Dictatorship of the Proletariat." The article is a valuable addition to and development of those ideas that are touched upon in *World Bolshevism*. It was published in the Marx "jubilee" issue of the magazine *Rabochii Internatsional* [The Workers' International], published under the editorship of Martov in Moscow in 1918.

F. Dan
November 1923

I.

The Roots of World Bolshevism

1. Bolshevism as a World Phenomenon

When the phrase "world Bolshevism" was first used in 1918, it seemed paradoxical to many Russian Marxists. It was absurd to think that our raw provincial Russian experience could prefigure the forms and content of the revolutionary process for "the rotten West."[1] We were all inclined to attribute Russian Bolshevism to the agrarian nature of the country, to the absence of deep political education among the broad masses, in a word, to purely national factors. It seemed extremely unlikely that the revolutionary movement in other countries—developing in significantly different social conditions—would take the ideological and political form of Bolshevism. At best, it was assumed that revolutions in similarly underdeveloped agrarian countries such as Romania, Hungary, and Bulgaria might become tinged with Bolshevism.

Likewise, it seemed obvious to western European socialists that Bolshevism was ill-suited for export on the world political market. Repeatedly they insisted that this purely Russian phenomenon could not take root in western Europe. Certainty on precisely this point was one of the reasons that prominent figures of European social democracy, by praising Russian Bolshevism, paved the way for the influence of Bolshevik ideas on the working masses of their own countries. They did not foresee that in their own countries, at a certain moment, Bolshevism would emerge "like a thief in the night." For reasons of mundane day-to-day politics, they either refused to make any criticism of the ideology and policy of Russian Bolshevism, or, without reservations, took it under their wing, protecting it from its bourgeois enemies. In doing so, they failed to separate the revolution as such from the specific phenomenon of Bolshevism, which incorporated a repudiation of the ideological heritage of the International.[2] Many representatives of western European socialism still follow this policy. Not long ago, when he clarified the reasons for his party's failure in the elections to the Constituent Assembly, [Karl] Kautsky chided its leaders for persistently avoiding public criticism of Russian Bolshevism and instead providing it with political publicity.[3]

Such an attitude, we repeat, was possible only insofar as western European socialists were guided by the slogan "that's not my headache" and were confident that it was not, in fact, their headache.

When, however, it became clear to everyone that "world Bolshevism" had everywhere become the most significant factor of the revolutionary process, western European Marxists turned out to be no less, if not more, unprepared than their Russian counterparts to understand the historical significance of this phenomenon and the roots that nourish it.

2. The Legacy of War

It became obvious after the experience of the first three months of revolution in Germany that Bolshevism was not *only* the product of an agrarian revolution.[4] In fact, there was every reason to reconsider that view—which had managed to acquire the strength of prejudice—after the experience of revolution in Finland.[5] Of course, the national characteristics of Bolshevism in Russia are largely explained by our agrarian relations. "World Bolshevism," however, must clearly be derived from other social factors.

The role that the *army* plays in social life, thanks to the world war, is without any doubt the first common factor that is manifested in the revolutionary processes of countries as socially different as Russia, Germany, England, and France. There is an undeniable connection between the role of soldiers in the revolution and the Bolshevik element in that revolution. Bolshevism is not simply a "soldiers' revolution," but the influence of Bolshevism on the course of the revolution in each country is proportional to the participation of armed soldier masses in this revolution.

The influence of the soldier and the army environment on the revolution in Russia was, in its time, adequately analyzed. From the very first days of the Bolshevik wave, Marxists identified the "communism of the consumer" as the only social interest binding together social elements very different in their class composition and even declassed—that is, detached from their natural social milieu.

Less attention was paid to another aspect of the social revolutionary psychology of the soldier masses: that is their peculiar "anti-parliamentarism"—quite understandable in a social environment not shaped, as in the past, through the school of collective defence of its interests, but in the present drawing its strength and influence exclusively from the possession of weapons.

English newspapers reported the following curious fact. When English troops on the French front were sent ballots during the most recent parliamentary elections, in many cases soldiers burned masses of them, stating, "When we return to England, we will put things right there." In both Germany and Russia we have seen many examples of how the soldier masses showed their first active interest in politics by expressing their desire to "put things right" through force of arms—whether that be "from the Right," as happened in the first months of the Russian revolution and the first weeks of the German one, or "from the Left." In both cases it is a question of a particular corporate consciousness nourished by the certainty that possession of weapons and the ability to use them makes it possible to control the destinies of the state. This outlook comes into fatal, irreconcilable conflict with the ideas of democracy and with parliamentary forms of government.

But despite the enormous role played by the soldier masses in shaping the Bolshevik element, this alone is insufficient to explain the success of Bolshevism or its ubiquity. In Russia, severe disappointment befell those who, in October 1917, with blissful optimism, declared Bolshevism to be "revolutionary praetorianism" and predicted that with the demobilization of the army the social roots of Bolshevism would disappear. On the contrary, the genuine features of Bolshevism were especially clearly manifested when the old army that had brought it to power had disappeared, replaced by a new armed force on which Bolshevism relied—an armed force that ceased to be a factor, or even a participant, in state administration. On the other hand, in both Finland and Poland—countries without national armies that have passed through the war—we have observed a Bolshevik element that is developing completely independently of any soldier's revolution.

Therefore, the ultimate roots of Bolshevism must be sought, in the final analysis, in the state of the proletariat.

3. The Psychology of Bolshevism

What are the essential features of proletarian Bolshevism as a world phenomenon?

The first is maximalism, that is, the desire for immediate, maximum results in the implementation of social improvements without any attention to objective conditions. This maximalism presupposes a dose of naive social optimism, the uncritical belief that such maximum results may be achieved at any time, that the resources and wealth of the society that the proletariat aspires to acquire are inexhaustible.

The second is a lack of attention to the requirements of social production—the predominance, as with the soldiers, of the consumer's point of view over that of the producer.

The third is the propensity to resolve all issues of political struggle, the struggle for power, by the direct application of armed force, even in relations between different sections of the proletariat. This propensity arises from a skeptical attitude toward the possibilities of finding a democratic solution to social and political problems. In the literature, the *objective* factors that account for the prevalence of these trends in the contemporary workers' movement have already been adequately clarified.

The working masses have changed qualitatively. The old cadres, the most class-educated, spent four and a half years at the front. Detached from productive work, they became permeated with the psychology of the trenches, spiritually dissolved into the social milieu of declassed elements. On their return to the ranks of the proletariat, they brought to it a revolutionary spirit but, at the same time, the spirit of soldiers' rabble-rousing. During the war, these class-educated cadres had been replaced in industry by millions of new workers drawn from ruined artisans and other "little people," rural proletarians, and working-class women. These new proletarians worked under conditions where the political movement of the proletariat had completely disappeared and the trade union movement had been reduced to pitiful dimensions. Despite the enormous growth of the war industry in Germany, it was not until the revolution that membership in the metalworkers' union returned to the level of July 1914. Class consciousness in these new proletarian masses developed extremely slowly, as they had almost no experience in collective struggle alongside more advanced strata of the working class.

While those who had lived in the trenches for many years lost their professional skills, were detached from regular productive labour, and were exhausted by the psychologically and physically inhuman conditions of modern warfare, the masses who took their place in the factories expended tremendous energy working overtime to acquire the bare necessities whose prices had increased massively. Most of this exhausting labour was carried out to produce means of destruction, labour that was, from the social point of view, unproductive and could not contribute to generating in the working masses the consciousness of the indispensability of their labour for the existence of society. But this consciousness constitutes an extremely essential element in the class psychology of the modern proletariat.

In all the countries directly or indirectly affected by the world war, these socio-psychological factors were the prerequisites facilitating the development of the Bolshevik element.

4. The Crisis of Proletarian Consciousness

Nevertheless, it seems to me that the factors indicated above are not enough to explain the progress made by the Bolshevik element in the world arena. If Bolshevism is putting down deep roots in the working masses not only in those countries that took part in the war but also in neutral countries, this is only because the ascendance of these factors did not encounter sufficient psychological resistance in the social and political skills and the ideological tradition of the broad masses of the proletariat.

As early as 1917–18, the same phenomenon could be seen in different countries. The working masses awakening to the class struggle showed extreme distrust for those workers' organizations that had led their movement up to August 1914. In Germany and Austria, strike movements took place against the decisions of the unions. Here and there influential clandestine groups were formed, and these took the lead in political and economic struggles. In England, factory committees arose in opposition to the trade unions and launched powerful strikes. The same phenomena could be observed in the neutral countries, such as the Scandinavian nations and Switzerland.

After the war ended and the hands of the proletariat were set free, this trend manifested itself with even greater force. In November and December 1918, there was a general desire among the broad masses in Germany to exclude the unions from any role in the leadership of the economic struggle and in the control of private production.

Soviets [councils] and factory committees strove to take their place.[6] The Haase-Ebert government had to reckon with this fact and, at the expense of the unions, extend responsibilities to these new organizational centres.[7] In England, the press noted that the most characteristic feature of the new strike movement was the masses' distrust of their trade union officials—the masses' refusal to submit to official directives. In one of his speeches in the House of Commons, [the United Kingdom's Prime Minister] Lloyd George specifically emphasized this point as one of particular concern to the government.

The class movement called into existence by the war raised up new, deeper strata of the proletarian mass, strata that had not yet passed through the long school of organized struggle. These new strata did not find the guidance of a solid bloc of advanced comrades, united by the commonality of their ends and means, their program and their tactics. Rather, they found the crumpled edifice of the old parties and unions, the old International experiencing the deepest crisis the working-class movement had ever known, an International torn apart by irreconcilable warring factions, an International shaken in its beliefs, beliefs that for decades had seemed immutable.

In these conditions, nothing other than what we are now witnessing could have been expected. The movement of new strata of the proletariat, and, partly, even of some who were already marching under the banner of social democracy in 1914, is developing as if in a vacuum in terms of ideological and political continuity. These new strata are spontaneously creating their own ideology, formed under the direct pressure of the relations and conditions *of the current moment*—a moment that is exceptional from the economic, political, and socio-psychological point of view. "Naked upon the bare earth" is very often how the proletariat appears today.[8] The mass proletarian movement was brought to a complete halt for four and a half years. The intellectual life of the working class completely atrophied. But was this not the case everywhere?

After all, *Burgfrieden*, that sacred union, involved the cessation of all agitation dealing with the irreconcilable class contradictions of society and the cessation of all educational and revolutionary work aimed at "socialization of consciousness."[9] The work of the sacred union was diligently supplemented by censorship and the regime of martial law. That is why, when the masses began to stir, bewildered after the crushing blow of the world war, they did not find at hand any ideological centre with universally recognized and undisputed moral authority, a centre on which they could psychologically find a "point of support." What they were offered was only the psychological freedom to choose between the various remnants of the old International. Is it surprising that they chose those which represented the most simplistic, most general expression of the spontaneous instinct of revolt, those which were the least attached to the bonds of ideological continuity, and could endlessly adapt themselves to the demands of the emerging strata? Is it surprising that the reciprocal action between these emerging strata and such ideological elements led to the creation of ideological *retrogression* in the workers' movements of the most advanced countries, that it led to a revival of illusions, prejudices, slogans, and methods of struggle that had had their place in the period of Bakuninism, at the beginning of the Lassallean movement, or even earlier—in the movements of the proletarian elements of the sans-culottes of Paris and Lyons in 1794 and 1797?[10]

The fourth of August 1914—the day the social democratic majority surrendered to imperialism—witnessed a catastrophic break in the continuity of the class movement of the proletariat. On that day, the germs of all these phenomena were already present, phenomena that still surprise many people today. In those gloomy days, the thoughtful observer should already have discerned, behind the two self-satisfied figures of Scheidemann and Vandervelde, a "laughing third" figure— *anarchism*, ready to be reborn from the soil of ideological devastation.[11]

In the very first weeks of the war, I had occasion to write that the crisis it caused in the working-class movement was primarily a "moral crisis": the loss of mutual trust between the various sections of the proletariat, the loss of faith within the proletarian masses in the old moral and political beliefs. For many decades, ideological bonds connected different sections of the movement—reformists and revolutionaries, at certain moments even socialists and anarchists—and all of the above with liberal and Christian workers. I could not imagine that the loss of mutual trust, the destruction of ideological bonds, would lead to a *civil war* among proletarians.[12] But it was clear to me that this prolonged, internal disintegration of class-based ideological unity, that this absence of a unifying ideology—which were consequences of the collapse of the International—would determine the whole picture of the reviving revolutionary movement. And it was because of the inevitability of these effects of the collapse of the International that revolutionary Marxists had the duty to work energetically to weld together the proletarian elements who had remained true to the class struggle and to react resolutely against "social-patriotism," even at a time when the masses had not yet awakened from nationalist frenzy and military panic. To the extent that it would have been possible to achieve this welding together on an international level, there could be hope that in the spontaneous risings of the future, the ideological legacy of a half century of workers' struggle would not sink without a trace and that it would be possible to build an ideological-organizational dam to contain the anarchist wave.

This was the objective meaning of the Zimmerwald-Kienthal approach of 1915 and 1916.[13] Unfortunately, the goal it set itself was far from realized. This failure must not be attributed, of course, either to accidents or to the mistakes of individual "Zimmerwaldists." Evidently, the crisis of the world labour movement was too deep for the efforts of the internationalist minorities of the time to change its course or to lessen the birth pangs of a new proletarian consciousness and new proletarian organizations. The very fact of this serves as proof of how historically inevitable the crisis was and how deeply its origins were rooted in profound changes in the historical existence of the proletariat, changes that had not yet resulted in corresponding changes in its collective consciousness.

"The owl of Minerva takes its flight only when the shades of night are gathering," Hegel said.[14] Classes only begin to realize the historical significance of their movement after they have completed a certain cycle in their development. This was the case historically for the movement of classes that preceded the proletariat. It is in the movement of the proletariat that theory, for the first time—while illuminating the movement's meaning as a link in the chain of historical development and the objective, historically necessary goals toward which it is going—has attempted to *direct* the movement so as to reduce to a minimum the number of victims and the loss of social energy that is characteristic of a "trial-by-error evolution." This theory managed to do a lot, but it could not do everything. Once again, the chaos of historical development has proven stronger than theory. Once again, it has been confirmed that as long as humanity has not made a "leap from the realm of necessity to the realm of freedom," as long as it has yet to subdue the elements of its own social economy, it is doomed to move mostly in darkness through its own trial-by-error efforts; to learn from defeats and the bitter fruits of retreats and zigzags.[15] More than is the case with the movement of any other class, the movement of the proletariat is imbued with elements of a conscious historical creativity. But, until the proletariat and the rest of humanity is the master of its own economic life, it will have to set very narrow limits to the possibilities of self-emancipation [*samoosvobozhdenie*]—of controlling the course of historical events with the aid of scientific theory. The depth of the collapse that occurred on 4 August 1914, its long duration and the endurance of its ideological consequences, show that at this stage of historical development, these limits are even narrower than we believed in our proud celebrations of the successes achieved by the international workers movement in the last quarter of a century, including the dominance within it of revolutionary Marxism.

The theoretical and political opponents of revolutionary teachings are rushing to gloat and proclaim, "the bankruptcy of Marxism." Do not be so hasty to declare victory. The very "defeat" of Marxism as the practical leader of the movement has revealed its greatest triumph as the "materialist interpreter" of history. As the ideology of the conscious section of the advanced class, Marxism has shown itself to be entirely subject to the basic law of development established by Marxist theory, which governs the evolution of all ideologies within an anarchic, class-divided society. Under the influence of the historical situation, Marxist theory evolved in the consciousness of one part of the working class into the "social patriotism" of class collaboration. In the consciousness of a different part of the working class, it evolved into a rudimentary anarcho-Jacobin "communism." But this differentiation is due precisely to *the supremacy of "being" over "consciousness,"* the material side of the historical process of development over ideology, a supremacy proclaimed by the teachings of Marx and Engels.

Only when the collective consciousness of the proletariat realizes the secret of its own misadventures during the present period of transition, only when it discovers for itself the historical reasons for yesterday's downfall and the objective meaning of its current wanderings—only then will it find the means to overcome the contradictions of its current movement, the utopianism of its immediate goals, and the limitation of its methods.

5. A Step Backward

The rupture in tradition, the loss of faith by the masses in the old leaders and the old organizations—this made it extremely easy to imbue the new revolutionary movement with those anarchistic ideological and psychological themes that now characterize it everywhere. The change in the social composition of the proletariat, the four-year school of war and the resulting degradation, coarsening, and "simplification" of the European spiritual physiognomy created fertile ground for the revival of ideas and methods thought to have been irrevocably outmoded.

The dominance of "consumer communism" over the intention to organize production on a collective basis—that is, disdain for the tasks of maintaining and ensuring the development of the forces of production—can now be seen everywhere among the proletarian masses. That is a great evil, one that marks a decisive step backward in the social development of the proletariat, in the process of its formation into a class capable of leading society. One of the principal tasks of

Marxist social democracy is to combat this trend of the revolutionary movement—a trend that so obviously feeds Bolshevism. But, while combating it, one should not lose sight of the perspectives of historical development. We should not forget the ground on which the popular masses acquired this disregard for the development of the forces of production. Over a four-year period, the ruling classes set about destroying the forces of production, destroying the accumulated social wealth, solving all the problems of maintaining economic life through the crude method of "plunder what has been plundered"—i.e., by requisitions, indemnities, confiscations, and forced labour imposed on the defeated.[16] Should we be astonished that, deprived of any political education for four years, the popular masses, when called upon to make history, began where the ruling classes left off? An examination of past revolutions makes it possible to assert that, in past centuries, extreme revolutionary parties also settled problems of economic policy with requisitions, confiscations, and indemnities, borrowing these methods from the arsenal of the wars of their time.

For years on end, the capitalist classes recklessly destroyed the forces of production, squandered the accumulated wealth, and diverted the best workers from their productive labour. They reassured themselves that this temporary destruction of the national heritage and its sources would (in the event of victory) lead to such a flourishing of the national economy through the conquest of world hegemony, annexations, and the like, that all the sacrifices would be repaid a hundredfold. None of the statesmen of the imperialist coalitions could furnish any serious evidence to support this opinion. Similarly, none of them could provide any serious arguments against the obvious truth that the world war, with its gigantic expense and destruction, would inevitably throw the world economy (or at least that of Europe) a considerable degree backward. In the end, these statesmen, as well as the bourgeois masses, shrugged off all their doubts in the naive belief that "everything would turn out all right" and that the elements of economic development would somehow heal the wounds inflicted by the "creativity" of the imperialist classes.

Is it any wonder that the working masses are also full of a similar unconscious faith when they try to radically improve their situation without taking into account the continuing destruction of the forces of production? The fatalism that overwhelmed the world bourgeoisie on the day it gave free rein to the monster of war in turn infected the popular masses. Insofar as they reflected on the consequences of anarchy, the masses also unconsciously hoped that the curve of historical development would end up leading them to their destination and that the complete victory of the working class over its opponents would, in and of itself, heal the wounds inflicted on the national economy by the struggle for this victory.

Insofar as this is so, the proletarian masses today stand only a little higher than the petit-bourgeois masses who made a revolution in England in the seventeenth century and in France in the eighteenth.[17] As then, the conscious struggle of these masses provides no guarantee that their efforts will result in the system to which they aspire, and not, in fact, in a completely different kind of system. This, of course, is a sad sign of retrogression within the workers' movement. The whole historical meaning of the immense work carried out by that movement since 1848 was to bring the conscious creativity of the proletariat in line with the laws of historical development that had been discovered, and thereby, for the first time in history, to ensure that the objective results of the revolutionary process were in line with the subjective aims pursued by the revolutionary class.[18]

Yes, it is a retrogression. But when this retrogression is denounced, and when right-wing socialists base their policy on denouncing it, we cannot forget that it was *with their assistance* that this retrogression was prepared. Where were they during the great war, when for the first time in history there was a need to teach humanity a lesson about respect for the forces of production? Did they not, tailing after the bourgeois patriots, convince the popular masses that by means of the systematic, intensive destruction of the [enemy country's] forces of production, within a certain time it would be possible to create the conditions for an unprecedented flourishing of these same forces in their own country?

"Through unlimited destruction, toward development at the highest level"—did not this slogan of the world war become the slogan of world Bolshevism?

This culture of disdain for the future of the national economy and for the maintenance of the forces of production—a disdain cultivated with the assistance of the right-wing socialists—permeates the whole psychology of the society that lived through the world war. This is true to such an extent that the social groups that today most fanatically oppose Bolshevism in the name of safeguarding and reconstructing these forces of production proceed regularly to employ means that are just as destructive from the economic point of view as are the methods of Bolshevism itself. We can observe this in both Ukraine and the Volga region, where the bourgeoisie preferred to destroy food stockpiles, railways, warehouses of supplies, and factory equipment rather than see them pass into the hands of the Bolsheviks. And, during the "sabotage" at the end of 1917, we observed how the right wing of democracy could denounce the Bolshevik revolution for economic vandalism while completely ignoring the blows that the successes of this "sabotage" would have inevitably inflicted on the national economy, much more than they would have inflicted on Bolshevik rule.[19]

We are now witnessing the same thing in Germany. There is perhaps no idea as popular in modern Germany as the idea that labour discipline is the only thing capable of saving the productive forces of the country. In the name of this idea, the bourgeois and right-wing socialist parties denounce the Spartacist elements of the proletariat for their tendency to provoke permanent strikes and to thus undermine any possibility of regular productive labour.[20] Objectively, they are right: the German economy is in such a critical state that a "strike epidemic" could in itself lead to a catastrophe. But what is interesting is that, when the bourgeoisie and the elements grouped around the right-wing socialists resist Bolshevism, it is increasingly by means of strikes. Recently, in the struggle against the Spartacist movement, "bourgeois strikes"—strikes of all the liberal professions as well as of state and local public servants—are becoming commonplace. All at the same moment, doctors and other medical personnel leave their hospitals, railway employees suspend rail traffic.

And the reasons they advance to justify these actions! Here in one of the eastern cities, the soldiers' council [soviet] decides to disarm a division whose mood it considers counter-revolutionary. An assembly of representatives of the bourgeois professions finds that the division has furnished proof of its loyalty to the republic. They protest against the disarmament as constituting a weakening of the eastern front in the face of a possible invasion by the Russian Bolsheviks. As a result of this, they decide to proclaim a strike until the Council [Soviet] annuls the decision. Cases of this kind are not uncommon.[21]

Obviously it was not Bolshevism—i.e., the "extremist" current of the far-left-wing tendency of the class movement of the proletariat—which gave rise to the triumph of the "consumerist" point of view over the "productivist" one. It was not Bolshevism that caused the neglect of the development of the forces of production and the consumption of the surplus economic wealth accumulated from past production. On the contrary, the growth of this tendency of the proletariat's class movement, so clearly opposed to the very spirit of Marxist socialism, is the consequence of the disease with which capitalist society was afflicted from the moment it was hit by the crisis. Historians of the future will therefore see the triumph of Bolshevik doctrines in the workers' movement of the advanced countries, not as a sign of an excess of revolutionary consciousness, but as proof of the proletariat's insufficient emancipation from the psychological atmosphere of bourgeois society.

It is for this reason that a policy that seeks to cure society of the economic vandalism of Bolshevism through an alliance with or capitulation to the bourgeoisie is a policy that is fundamentally false. We have seen in Russia—in Ukraine, in Siberia—that, after having defeated the Bolsheviks by force of arms, the bourgeoisie has been unable to put an end to the economic devastation. In Europe, we are already seeing that, if it succeeds in defeating the proletarian revolution—in spite of all "League of Nations" labels—the bourgeoisie will construct such a system of international relations, such a body of armour on the economic organism, such customs barriers, that the national economy will be condemned to reconstitute itself on the volcano of new armed conflicts, threatening even greater devastation than that which the world has just experienced. In these conditions, it is more than doubtful that the world bourgeoisie will be able to bring Europe back to the level of economic development from which it was toppled by the war. Either the victory of reason over chaos within the framework of the proletarian revolution or economic and cultural regression for a fairly long period: there can be no other outcome from the present situation.

Typical of the movement whose ideology is world Bolshevism is a disregard for the production apparatus bequeathed from the old society. Accompanying this is a similar disdain for the *intellectual* culture of the old society, a readiness in the revolutionary process to ignore the positive elements of this culture. Here, too, the masses, now entering the historical arena as creators of the revolution, stand an entire stage below those masses that represented the core of the class movement of the proletariat in the previous peaceful era. And here, too, there can be no doubt that this retrogression must be entirely attributed to the influence of the four-year war.

In 1794, on the occasion of the execution of Lavoisier, the sans-culottes of Paris were already saying, "The Republic does not need scientists!" Robespierre, supporting the choice of [Jean-Paul] Marat over the English materialist philosopher [Joseph] Priestley as the Paris delegate to the National Convention, declared that there were "too many philosophers" in the representative assemblies.[22] Modern sans-culottism in its communist sense is not so far removed from these examples in its attitude to the scientific heritage bequeathed by bourgeois society. But then again, it is only "scribes and Pharisees" who can be outraged by this and not remember the militarism whose orgies only yesterday they celebrated, before which they bowed down, or to which they cowardly surrendered. Need it be recalled that militarism hardly treated science and philosophy any better, and that it is they who cultivated the contempt for science and philosophy among the popular masses who are now trying to make history. If German and French militarism pitilessly sent professors and scientists to dig trenches and to contribute their clerical labour to the great cause of the "defence of the fatherland" without worrying about the temporary decline in the country's intellectual productivity, what right have we to be indignant if, in an identical spirit of irrational waste, professors and scientists are used to clean cesspools or dig graves for the dead?

To the people who were indignant over the German troops' destruction of the marvellous Reims Cathedral, Bernard Shaw sarcastically said, "You cannot have both a 'beautiful' war and beautiful monuments of art." A. V. Lunacharsky came to the same conclusion on his own— that one cannot keep in one's heart the cult of "beautiful" civil war and care for the beautiful Basil the Blessed.[23]

The best people of the European bourgeoisie—the Norman Angells and Romain Rollands—warned the old society against the devastating consequences, for economic and intellectual culture, of an imperialist war.[24] They were ridiculed by rabid gangs of bourgeois chauvinists or even denounced as backstabbers and traitors. A society intoxicated by patriotism gloated at their isolation. Is it any wonder that the "patriots" of the revolutionary element see Kautsky and the like—with their appeals to the proletariat to adopt a careful attitude to the economic and cultural resources that have escaped the catastrophe—as ridiculous pedants? Intoxicated by their successes, the most ardent [of the revolutionary patriots] deem the most frank to be "backstabbers and traitors."

"You wanted it, you wanted it, George Dandin. [... You got just what you deserve]."[25] In 1914–15, the bourgeoisie proved its still inexhaustible power of influence over the working class. It showed that the intellectual world of the proletariat was still subordinate to it. Today, the bourgeoisie is up against a working class that is itself shaped by four years of "wartime" education that led to the degeneration of a proletarian culture that had been developed over long decades of class struggle.

There was fertile soil within the working masses of the advanced capitalist countries for the new heyday of the unsophisticated [pre-Marxist] communist ideas of equal distribution that prevailed in the labour movement at the beginning of its development. That is precisely why, at this stage of the revolution, the role of inspirer and hegemon of the revolution could be assumed by the country where the roots of this simplistic conception of socialism go deep into the soil of primary accumulation and primordial social relations untouched by capitalist culture.

Imperialism brought western Europe back to the economic and cultural level of the European East. Should it be a surprise that the latter is now imposing its ideological forms on the revolutionized masses of the West? World Bolshevism, which the European bourgeois and social-nationalists regard with apocalyptic horror, is perhaps the first gift from the East to triumphant imperialism of the West, a gift of revenge for the devastation and arrested economic development caused by the West.

II.

The Ideology of "Sovietism"

6. The Mysticism of the Soviet System

The political ideology of that part of the contemporary social-revolutionary movement that has taken on the colouring of Bolshevism recognizes only soviets as the form of political organization by which the social emancipation of the proletariat can take place.

The soviet state structure, leading to the gradual abolition of the state as an apparatus of social coercion, from this point of view appears to be the historically conditioned product of a lengthy social development, a social form growing out of the class contradictions of capitalism when these have become acute at the highest imperialistic stage of its development. As the most suitable form for the class dictatorship of the proletariat, the soviet structure is seen as the most perfect form of genuine democracy, one that corresponds to the stage of development of society when the old bourgeois democracy has completely exhausted itself.

However, every perfection has a dangerous characteristic. That part of humanity untroubled by critical reasoning, completely disregarding the nuances of "grey [drab] theory," becomes impatient to adopt perfection, without taking note that the perfection in question is supposed to be based on particular historical prerequisites. The metaphysical

thinking of the common masses has absolutely no regard for the dialectical negation of the absolute. It does not know the category of relativity.
Once the true, authentic, and perfect form of social life has at last been
discovered, it insists on making this perfect form a reality.

And we see how this "perfection"—the soviet form of democracy—
turns out, contrary to theory, to be suitable for all peoples and societies,
no matter their stage of social development. All that is necessary is that
the people concerned should desire to modify the structure of the state
system under which they are suffering. The soviet form of organization
becomes the political slogan for the proletariat of the most developed
industrial countries—the United States, England, Germany—as well
as for overwhelmingly agricultural Hungary, peasant Bulgaria, and for
Russia, where agriculture is just emerging from the stage of subsistence.

But the universal efficacy of the soviet form of organization does
not end there. Communist publicists write seriously of soviet overturns
emerging in Asiatic Turkey, among the Egyptian fellahin, and in the
pampas and grasslands of South America. In Korea, the founding of a
soviet republic is apparently only a matter of time, while in India, China,
and Persia the soviet idea is apparently advancing with the speed of an
express train. As for the Bashkirs, Kyrgyz, and Turkmen of Turkestan
and the mountain dwellers of Dagestan, it is well-known that the soviet
system has already been grafted onto the primordial, undeveloped conditions of their social lives.

Contrary to Marxist theory, which originally provided its justi-
fication, the soviet form of organization turns out to be a universal
state form that can solve any problems and contradictions of social
development, not only those of highly developed capitalism, characterized by extreme intra-national antagonisms between the proletariat
and the bourgeoisie. In theory, peoples entering into soviet statehood
are expected to have in fact, or at least in their thinking, passed through
the stage of bourgeois democracy. They are expected to have freed
themselves from a number of illusions: parliamentarism, the need
for the "four-tails" [universal, direct, equal, and secret] of suffrage,
the need for freedom of the press, etc.[1] Only then can they know the

supreme perfection of soviet statehood. In practice, however, peoples skip through all the stages, possessed by the metaphysical negation of any relatively progressive categories. Kyrgyz nomads, Brazilian shepherds, and Egyptian fellahin resolve: "[But let your communication be] Yea, yea; Nay, nay: for whatsoever is more than these cometh of social betrayal."[2] If soviets are the perfect form of the state, if they are the key to the destruction of social inequality and poverty, then who would willingly put on the yoke of less perfect forms so that, through painful practice, they could learn their contradictions? Having tasted the sweet, who would wish to taste the bitter?[3]

In February 1918, at Brest-Litovsk, Trotsky and [Lev] Kamenev, with great tenacity, defended the principle of self-determination of peoples.[4] They demanded from victorious Germany that this principle be applied—through *universal and equal suffrage*—in Poland, Lithuania, and Latvia. The relative historic value of democracy was still recognized at that time. A year later, however, at the congress of the Russian Communist Party, the intrepid [Nikolai] Bukharin was already demanding that the principle of "self-determination of peoples" be replaced with the principle of "self-determination of the working classes."[5] Vladimir Lenin succeeded in maintaining the principle of self-determination—for underdeveloped peoples—just as some philosophers who, not wanting to quarrel with the church, would limit the scope of their materialist teachings to animals deprived of the benefits of divine grace. The Communist congress refused to follow Bukharin, not because of doctrinal hesitations, but because of considerations of a *diplomatic* nature, considerations that were expressed by Lenin: it was thought unwise to alienate from the Communist International the Hindus, Persians, and other peoples who, as yet deprived of grace, were in a situation of nationwide struggle against the foreign oppressor. In essence, of course, the Communists were in full agreement with Bukharin. Having tasted the sweet, who would offer their neighbour the bitter?

When the Turkish consul in Odessa put out an unsubstantiated story about the triumph of a soviet revolution in the Ottoman

Empire, not one Russian newspaper refused to take seriously this obvious canard. Not a single publication expressed the slightest skepticism concerning the ability of the brave Turks to jump over the stages of self-determination, the "four-tails" [universal, direct, equal, and secret] of suffrage, bourgeois parliamentarism, etc. The hoax was completely successful.

Because mysticism provides a breeding ground for hoaxes. The very concept of a political form that, by virtue of its particular character, can surmount all economic, social, and national contradictions, in the midst of which advances the revolution, generated by the world war—this is nothing less than mystical.

The congress of the Independent Social Democratic Party of Germany at Leipzig, where its members puzzled over how to reconcile "All power to the soviets!" with the foundations of a democratic system and with the traditional ideas of social democracy concerning the political forms of the socialist revolution, showed once again how profoundly today's popular idea—that of "All power to the soviets!"—is imbued with social mysticism.

The mystery escapes the understanding of the revolution's true believers with the same persistence that the mystery of the immaculate conception escapes the understanding of the Christian faithful.

Sometimes it escapes the understanding of its own creator. We got the news that the soviet idea had triumphed in Hungary. It seemed, at first, that everything had been done "according to the ritual." But one essential detail was missing. It was reported that the Hungarian "soviet" did not come into being as a result of a civil war within the Hungarian proletariat (we shall see later how important this detail is). It was, on the contrary, the product of the unity of the Hungarian proletariat. In a telegram, the complete text of which appeared in the foreign press, an astonished Lenin asked [Hungarian Communist leader] Béla Kun: "What proof do you have that your revolution is truly communist, and not merely socialist, that is to say (!) a revolution of social-traitors?"[6]

Béla Kun's reply, published in the Russian press, was evasive and betrayed some embarrassment. He reported that power rested in the hands of a group of five persons—two Communists, two Social Democrats, and "the fifth in the same category as your Lunacharsky." The mystery had grown deeper.

As a result of the extreme class antagonism between the proletariat and the bourgeoisie, the proletariat overthrows the highest forms of democratic statehood. The proletariat creates thereby a political form that is the specific expression of the dictatorship of the proletariat. This is the starting point of the "soviet idea." But the final point in the development of the "soviet idea" is that it is a political form universally applicable to all sorts of social upheavals, a political form that embraces all the diverse content of the revolutionary movements of the twentieth century.

In this dialectical contradiction, the mystery of "sovietism" is revealed, a mystery before which dogmatic political thinking on both the Left and the Right is powerless.

7. Dictatorship of a Minority

The mechanism by which people's revolutions unfolded in the preceding historical period had the following characteristics. The active factors in the social upheavals were *minorities* of those social classes in whose interest the various phases of the revolution were carried out. These minorities made use of the vague discontent and sporadic explosions of anger arising among the dispersed masses of their respective classes, carrying the masses along the path of overturning the old social relations. At the same time, these active minorities made efforts to overcome the inertia [of the majority] through the concentrated energy [of the active minority] and, sometimes successfully, to crush the passive resistance of these same masses when the latter refused to move forward toward the broadening and deepening of the revolution. A dictatorship of an active revolutionary minority, a dictatorship that sometimes took on a terrorist character, was the natural result of the situation bequeathed by the old social order to the broad masses of the people, now called on by the revolution to actively make their own history.

Where the active revolutionary minority was not able to organize such a dictatorship or maintain it for some time, as was the case in Germany, Austria, and France in 1848, we observed the incompleteness of the revolutionary process, the incompleteness of the revolutions.

As Engels put it, the revolutions of the previous historical period were the work of conscious minorities exploiting the spontaneous outrage of majorities lacking consciousness.

Of course, the word "conscious" should be understood here in a relative sense. It was a question of pursuing certain political and social goals, however contradictory and utopian they may have been. The ideology guiding the Jacobins in 1793–94 was completely imbued with utopianism. It cannot be considered to have been the product of an awareness of the objective process of historical development. But in relation to the mass of peasants, small producers, and workers in whose name they demolished the Old Regime, the Jacobins represented a conscious vanguard whose destructive work was subordinate to definite positive objectives.

In the 1890s, Engels arrived at the conclusion that the epoch of revolutions effected by masses lacking consciousness under the leadership of conscious minorities had closed forever. From now on, he believed, revolution would be prepared by decades of political, organizational, and cultural work by socialist parties and would be carried out actively and consciously by the interested masses themselves.

Without question, this idea of Engels's was assimilated by the great majority of modern socialists—assimilated to such an extent that the slogan "All power to the soviets!" was originally launched as an answer to the question: During the revolutionary period, how does one ensure the most active, conscious, and self-active [samodeiatel'ni] participation of the masses themselves in all the processes of social creativity?

Read Lenin's articles and speeches of 1917 and you will discover this basic motif: "All power to the soviets!" means . . .

+ the direct, self-active [*samodeiatel'ni*] participation of the masses in the whole process of managing production and public affairs;

+ the obliteration of all forms of mediation between those who govern and those who are governed, the obliteration of all social hierarchy;

+ the maximum possible erasure of the boundaries between legislative and executive powers, between the apparatus of production and the apparatus of administration, between the national state machinery and the machinery of local self-government;

+ the maximum freedom of action for the masses with a minimum of autonomy for their elected representatives;

+ the complete abolition of all bureaucracy.

Parliamentarism was repudiated not only as the arena where two enemy classes collaborate politically and engage in "peaceful" combat, but also as a mechanism of public administration. And this repudiation was motivated, above all, by the contradiction that arises between this mechanism and the unlimited revolutionary self-activity [*samodeiatel'nost*] of the masses and their direct participation in government and production.

In August 1917, Lenin wrote:

The workers, having conquered political power, will smash the old bureaucratic apparatus, tear it down to its foundations, leaving no stone unturned, and replace it with a new one, consisting of the same workers and salaried employees, against whose transformation into bureaucrats *immediate* measures will be taken that were specified in detail by Marx and Engels: (1) not only election, but also recall at any time; (2) pay not to exceed that of a worker's wage; (3) immediate transition to ensuring that *everyone* performs the functions of control and supervision, so that *everyone* becomes a bureaucrat for a time and that, therefore, no one may become [an actual] bureaucrat.

"Since the majority of the people suppress their oppressors," he writes, "a 'special force' for suppression is no longer necessary.... Instead of the special institutions of a privileged minority (privileged bureaucracy, commanders of the standing army), the majority can directly fulfil all these functions, and the more the functions of state power are performed by the people as a whole, the less need there is for the existence of this power."[7]

Elsewhere, he wrote of the "substitution of a [*universal*] *people's militia* for the police" as well as proposing that "judges and other officials, both civil and military ... be elected by the people with the right to recall any of them at any time by decision of a majority of their electors."[8] He wrote of "workers' control" in its original sense, and of the direct participation of the people in the courts, not only in the form of a jury trial but also in the form of abolishing specialized prosecutors and defence counsels and by deciding questions of guilt through [the vote of] all present. That is how the overcoming of old bourgeois democracy through the soviet system was interpreted in theory—and sometimes in practice.

The first constitution, which was adopted at the Third Congress of Soviets on the initiative of V. Trutovskii, implemented the conception of "All power to the soviets!" when it gave comprehensive authority to the *volost'* soviet within the *volost'* [subdistrict or county], to the *uezd* soviet within the *uezd* [district], and to the *guberniia* soviet within the *guberniia* [province], while the coordinating functions of each of the higher soviet organs were limited exclusively to settling differences among the bodies/organs subordinated to it.[9]

Anticipating the objection that such extreme federalism might undermine national unity, Lenin wrote in *The State and Revolution*, the same pamphlet cited earlier:

Only those who are imbued a with petit-bourgeois superstitious faith in the state can assume that the destruction of the bourgeois state machine means the destruction of centralism! Now if the proletariat and the poor peasants take state power into their own hands, *organize themselves quite freely in communes*, and unite all the communes in striking at capital, in crushing the resistance of the capitalists, in transferring the privately owned railways, factories, land, and everything else to the entire nation, to the whole of society, won't that be centralism?[10]

Reality has cruelly shattered all these illusions. The "soviet state" has not established the practice of either election or recall of public officials and commanding staff. It has not abolished the professional police. It has not dissolved the courts into the direct law-making of the masses. It has not done away with social hierarchy in production. It has not destroyed the coercive power of the [national] state over the individual communes. On the contrary, in its development the soviet state displays the opposite tendency. In its behaviour, it displays a tendency toward intensified centralism of the state, a tendency toward the utmost possible strengthening of the principles of hierarchy and coercion. It displays a tendency toward the development of an entire specialized apparatus of repression. It displays a tendency toward greater independence of elective bodies from the control of the electoral masses. It displays a tendency toward total freedom of the executive organs from the representative institutions that appoint them. The "power of the soviets" has been realized in life as "Soviet Power," a power that originated in the soviets but has steadily become independent from the soviets.

We must assume that the Russian ideologists of the system have not abandoned their idea that a stateless social order should be the goal of the revolution. But as they see matters now, the road to this stateless social order no longer lies in the progressive "withering away" of the functions and institutions forged in the process of the development of the bourgeois state, as they said they had imagined in 1917. Now it appears that the road to this stateless social order lies in the expansion of these functions and in the revival, in an altered form, of many of the state institutions typical of the bourgeois era. They continue to reject democratic parliamentarism; however, they no longer reject along with it those instruments of state power to which parliamentarism is a partial counterbalance within bourgeois society: a counterbalance to the bureaucracy, the police, the standing army with a command staff independent of the soldiers, courts that are beyond the control of the community, and so on.

The transitional revolutionary state, according to theory, in contrast to the bourgeois state, should be an organ for the "coercion of the minority by the majority"—an organ of majority rule [*vlast*]. In reality, it turned out to be the same organ of minority rule [*vlast*] (of a different minority, of course).

Realization of this fact leads to an open or covert replacement of the power of the soviets [councils] with the power of a particular *party*. Little by little, the party becomes the principal state institution, the core of the entire system of the "republic of soviets [councils]."

The evolution accomplished by the idea of the "soviet state" in Russia sheds light on the psychological roots of the emergence of this idea in other countries, where the revolutionary process of today is as yet in its initial phase.

The "soviet system" turns out to be a means of putting in place and maintaining in power a revolutionary minority that seeks to defend those interests of the majority that the latter either has not recognized as its own or has not recognized as its own sufficiently so as to defend them with maximum energy and determination.

That this is so, is demonstrated by the fact that in many countries—as also happened in Russia—the idea of "Soviet Power" is used against the existing, real soviets [councils] that were created during the first manifestations of the revolution. It is thus directed, first and foremost, against the majority of the working class and against the political tendencies that dominated within the proletariat at the beginning of the revolution. Thus, the idea of "Soviet Power"—in terms of its actual political content—becomes an alias for the dictatorship of an extreme *minority of the proletariat.*

This is so true that when the failure of 3 July 1917 [the so-called July Days] demonstrated the stubborn resistance of the soviets to the onslaught of Bolshevism, Lenin disclosed the [truth about the] alias in his pamphlet *On Slogans* and proclaimed that the slogan "All power to the soviets!" was henceforth out of date and had to be replaced with the slogan "All power to the Bolshevik Party."[11]

But this "materialization" of the symbol, this disclosure of its true content, proved to be only a moment in revolutionary development, one that continued to take place under the sign of the "mystical" idea of the perfect political form, "at last discovered," a political form possessing the capacity to reveal the social essence of the proletarian revolution.[12]

Power held by the minority of a given class (or an alliance [of classes]) organized into a party in the name of the real interests of the class (or classes), is in no way something new, arising from antagonisms of the most recent phase of capitalism, fundamentally distinguishing the new revolutions from the old ones. On the contrary, the dictatorship by such a minority is *something common* to both, that makes today's revolution similar to those of the preceding historical period. If rule by a minority is the basic principle of the governmental mechanism in question, it is of little importance that—due to historical circumstances—this principle has assumed the form of soviets.

Indeed. The events of 1792–94 in France offer an example of a revolution that was realized by means of a minority dictatorship in the form of the dictatorship of the Jacobin party. The Jacobin party embraced the most active, the most "left-leaning," elements of the petite bourgeoisie, the proletariat, the declassed intelligentsia, and the lumpen proletariat. It exercised its dictatorship through a network of various institutions: communes, sections, clubs, and revolutionary committees. In this network, informal organizations established by workers in industry, of a type similar to our workers' soviets, were completely absent. Otherwise, however, among the network of institutions that implement the dictatorship of the minority, we see institutions that are similar to those of the Jacobin dictatorship. The party cells of today differ in no way from the Jacobin Clubs. The revolutionary committees of 1794 and 1919 are entirely alike. Today's *komitety bednoty* [committees of the poor peasants] are analogous to the committees and clubs on which the Jacobin dictatorship based itself in the villages, building them mainly among the poor elements.[13] Workers' soviets, factory committees, and trade-union centres leave their mark on the revolutions of our time, giving them their specific character. This, of course, reflects the influence that the proletariat in heavy industry now has on the content and course of the revolution. Nevertheless, such specifically class-based organizations, such purely proletarian formations, having grown from a modern industrial milieu, serve as the mechanical instruments for the dictatorship of a certain party minority, much as did the auxiliaries of the Jacobin dictatorship in 1792–94, though with completely different roots.

In the specific conditions of contemporary Russia, this party dictatorship primarily reflects the interests and sentiments of the proletarian sections of the population. This will be even more the case when soviet soviet power is consolidated in the more advanced industrial countries. But the decisive factor is not the nature of the soviets or their connections to industrial units. After 3 July 1917, we saw that Lenin envisaged the *direct* dictatorship of the Bolshevik Party, thereby bypassing the soviets. We see now that in some places such a dictatorship is fully realized through the channel of revolutionary committees and party cells. All of this does not prevent it from retaining the strongest connection with the proletariat, in class terms reflecting above all the interests and aspirations of the urban working class.

On the other hand, as an organizational form, the soviets can be filled with a different class content, since soviets of soldiers and peasants appear on the stage alongside the workers' soviets. Accordingly, in countries that are economically less developed than Russia, the Soviet Power may represent something other than the proletariat. It may represent the party dictatorship of a section of the peasantry, or other non-proletarian section of the population. This is the solution to the mystery of the "soviet system." A form derived from the specific features of a working-class movement corresponding to the highest development of capitalism proves equally suitable for countries without either large-scale capitalist production or a powerful domestic bourgeoisie, or a proletariat that has gone through the school of the class struggle—it is suitable for Egypt, for Yugoslavia, for Brazil, even for Korea.

In other words, in the developed countries, the proletariat has recourse to a soviet form of dictatorship from the moment its movement toward a social revolution encounters the impossibility of exercising its power except in the form of the *dictatorship of a minority*, a minority within the proletariat itself.

The theory of the "form at last discovered," the theory of the political form that, while belonging to the specific conditions of the imperialist phase of capitalism, is the only form that can realize the social emancipation of the proletariat, constitutes the historically necessary illusion through which the revolutionary segment of the proletariat renounces its belief in its ability to lead the majority of the population of the country and resurrects the forms of the *Jacobin dictatorship of a minority*, created by the bourgeois revolution of the eighteenth century—a revolutionary method that had been rejected by the working class to the extent that it had freed itself from the spiritual heritage of petit-bourgeois revolutionism. As soon as the soviet system has played its role as an alias under the cover of which the Jacobin and Blanquist idea of a minority dictatorship is reborn in the ranks of the proletariat, then the soviet system acquires a universal character, universally applicable to any kind of revolutionary upheaval.[14] All specific content associated with a definite phase of capitalist development is necessarily eliminated. The soviet system now becomes a *universal form of revolution, supposedly suitable to any revolution regardless of political divisions, inactivity, and lack of internal cohesion among the masses, provided only that the bases of the old regime have been radically undermined through the course of historical development.*

8. Dictatorship over the Proletariat

So, the secret of the triumph of the [idea of the] "soviet system" in the consciousness of the agitated proletarian masses of Europe lies in the loss of faith—by these revolutionary masses—in their ability to directly lead the majority of the people on the road to socialism. Since this popular majority, currently opposing socialism either actively or passively—or as yet continuing to follow parties that reject socialism—includes significant strata of the proletariat, the principle of the "soviet system" implies not only the rejection of democracy in the framework of the nation but also its elimination within the working class itself.

In theory, soviet rule does not abolish democracy, but only limits its scope to the working class and the "poorest peasantry." After all, the essence of democracy is not expressed—either exclusively or in principle—by absolute universal suffrage. The "universal" suffrage that we managed to win in the most advanced bourgeois countries before the Russian Revolution excluded women, the military, and sometimes young people up to the age of twenty-five. These exceptions did not render undemocratic these countries' systems, as long as among those called on to exercise the people's sovereignty, there existed a degree of democracy consistent with the preservation of the capitalist foundations of the social system.

For this reason, excluding from the circle of voters all bourgeois, rentiers, those who use hired labour, and even members of the liberal professions—something Plekhanov famously accepted for the period of the dictatorship of the proletariat—does not in itself make the soviet system something absolutely opposed to democracy.[15] On the contrary, such exceptions are entirely compatible with the development of other, no less significant principles of democracy. In spite of the limitation of electoral rights, this system is still a "more perfect democracy" than all the democratic regimes we have known to date, which have been based on the social domination of the [subordinate classes by the] bourgeoisie.

The exclusion of the bourgeois minority from participation in state power may be (as we think) both useless from the point of view of consolidating the power of the majority and directly harmful, since it leads to an impoverishment of the process through which the social content of the popular will is expressed in the electoral struggle.[16] But that alone does not eradicate the democratic character of the soviet system.

That democratic character is eradicated when the basic features of democracy are suppressed in the relations between citizens who stand inside the privileged circle, designated as the bearers of state power.

[Consider the following:]

+ Absolute subordination of the executive apparatus to popular representation (even though, in the case of the soviets, popular representation does not include all citizens).

+ The right to elect and recall the administration, judges, the police. Democracy within the army.

+ The control and open, public character of all administrative acts.

+ Freedom to form voluntary groupings of citizens (though this may mean freedom only for the "privileged," in the above-mentioned sense of the term).

+ Inviolability of citizens' individual and collective rights and protection from any abuses on the part of any individuals in power or official institutions.

+ Freedom of citizens to discuss all matters of state. The right of citizens to freely exert pressure on the governmental mechanism, etc., etc.

These are the integral features of a democratic regime, no matter how limited the circle of citizens to whom they apply. (After all, we have historical examples of democratic republics of slaveholders—Athens, for example.)

The theoreticians of the soviet system have never rejected these features of democracy as applicable to the internal system of the soviets. On the contrary, they argued that, given the restricted electoral base of the soviets, these principles would develop as they never could on the broader electoral base of capitalist democracies. Let us recall Lenin's promise about the participation of all working people in government, of all soldiers in the election of officers, and the abolition of all police and of all bureaucracy. The rejection of all democratism *within* the soviet system presupposes a recognition by those sections of the proletariat advocating such a rejection that either the working class forms a minority in a population that is hostile to it, or that it is deeply divided into factions fighting among themselves for power—or both.

In all these cases, the true essence of the popularity of the soviet system is found in the desire to ensure that the will of a certain revolutionary minority prevails, by suppressing the will of all other groups of the population, including proletarian groups.

Describing the fascination with the idea of the soviets that swept through the *Swiss* proletariat, Charles Naine, the well-known Swiss socialist, writes:

> At the beginning of 1918, there was genuine excitement. In Switzerland, without delay, soviets of worker, soldier and peasant deputies had to be formed, and a red guard established. It was up to the conscious minority to impose its will on the majority, by brute force if necessary. The great mass of workers was in such economic bondage, it was impossible for them to liberate themselves through their own efforts. Moreover, educated and trained by their masters, they were incapable of understanding their real interests. It was up to the conscious minority to free the masses from this tutelage. Only then would the masses be able to understand. Scientific socialism being the truth itself, the minority possessing the knowledge of this truth had a duty to impose it on the masses. Parliament is nothing more than an obstacle, an instrument of reaction. The bourgeois press, which poisons the minds of the people, must be suppressed, or at least muzzled. Freedom and democracy can only be revived later, after the socialist dictators have transformed the regime. Then the citizens will be able to form a true democracy, because they will be freed from the economic regime that oppresses them and keeps them from manifesting their true will.[17]

One has to be a hypocrite or completely oblivious not to see that Charles Naine has presented here, freed from verbal adornments, the true ideology of Bolshevism. It has been assimilated in this form by the masses in our country [Russia], Germany, Hungary—wherever the Bolshevik movement has made its appearance.

Verbal adornments do not always help to obscure this essence of the matter. Take, for example, the article by P. Orlovskii[18] in *Pravda*, no. 101, 13 May 1919, entitled "The Communist International and the World Soviet Republic." The author, in his own words, deals with "the very essence of the matter"—that is, with the soviet system. "The soviet system," he writes, "in itself means only the participation of the masses in public administration, but it does not assure them either dominance or even preponderant influence."[19]

In this tirade, if we substitute the words "parliamentary democracy" for the words "soviet system," we get the same elementary truth as the one expressed by Orlovskii. After all, while democratic parliamentarism, implemented consistently, ensures the participation of the masses in public administration, it does not in itself guarantee their political dominance.

What conclusion does Orlovskii draw from this?

"Only," he says, "when actual state power in the soviet system passes into the hands of the Communists, that is to say the party of the working class, will workers and the exploited not merely obtain access to state power, but also have an opportunity to rebuild the state on new principles that meet their needs," and so on.

In other words, the soviet system is good only insofar as it is in the hands of the Communists. For:

> As soon as the bourgeoisie succeeds in getting its hands on the soviets (as was the case in Russia under Kerensky and now—in 1919—in Germany), it will use them to fight against the revolutionary workers and peasants, just as the tsars used the soldiers, who came from the people, to oppress the people. Therefore, soviets can fulfil a revolutionary role—that is, to free the working masses— only when the Communists play the leading role. And for the same reason, the growth of soviet institutions in other countries is a revolutionary phenomenon in the proletarian sense—not merely in the petit-bourgeois sense—only when this growth goes hand in hand with the triumph of communism.[20]

It is impossible to express it more clearly. The "soviet system" is the scaffolding by which "state power passes into the hands of the Communists." The scaffolding is removed as soon as it has fulfilled its historic mission. While never spoken out loud, this is, in fact, what is done in real life.

At the same time, the premise is always: "The Communist Party, *that is to say*, the party of the working class." Not one of their parties, nor even the most advanced party best representing the general class interests of the proletariat, but *the only* truly working-class party.

Orlovskii's idea is well-illustrated in the resolutions adopted by the Communist conference at Kashin, published in *Pravda*, no. 3, 1919:

> The middle peasants may be admitted (!) to power, even when they do not belong to the party, if they accept the soviet platform—with the reservation that the leading and dominant role in the soviets must remain with the party of the proletariat. It is *to be seen as totally unacceptable* and dangerous to leave the soviets entirely in the hands of the non-party middle peasantry. That would expose all the achievements of the proletarian revolution to the danger of complete destruction at a moment when the decisive and final struggle with international reaction is taking place.[21]

To be sure, the Communists at Kashin reveal the secret meaning of "dictatorship" only insofar as it is applied to the peasantry. But, as everyone knows, the question of the dictatorship of the "middle worker" (there is such a term) is solved in the same manner. This is precisely the essence of "worker and peasant" power and not merely workers' power.

No doubt, what originally made "sovietism" so attractive to socialists was their utmost *confidence* in the collective intelligence of the working class, their confidence in the workers' ability to attain, by means of their dictatorship over the bourgeoisie, a condition of complete *self-governance*, without the shadow of *tutelage by a minority*. The first enthusiasm for the soviet system was an enthusiasm for escaping the framework of a hierarchically organized state.

In the eloquent report presented by Ernest Däumig (Left Independent)[22] at the first Pan-German Congress of Councils (16–21 December 1918), we read:

> The current German revolution has damnably little confidence in its own strength. Naturally, the spirit of military subservience and passive obedience still weighs heavily on it, a legacy of centuries. This spirit cannot be killed by electoral struggle or by election leaflets distributed among the masses every two or three years. It can only be killed by a sincere and powerful effort to maintain the German people in a condition of permanent political activity. And this can only be accomplished in the soviet [council] system. We must finish, once and for all, with all the old administrative machinery of the empire, of the individual [German] states and municipalities. *Self-governance*, instead of governance from above, should more and more become the aim of the German people.

And at the same congress, the Spartacist Heckert declared:

> The Constituent Assembly will be a *reactionary institution* even if it has a socialist majority, precisely because the German people are a completely apolitical people who want to be led and who have not shown any evidence of a desire to take their destinies into their own hands. Here in Germany, we wait to have liberty brought to us by leaders, not from the bottom up.

"The soviet system," he says elsewhere, "is the one that transfers *direct responsibility* for building society to the broad masses of the proletariat, while the Constituent Assembly is an organization that transfers this responsibility to the hands of the leaders."

But here's the interesting thing. In the same report in which Däumig glorifies the soviets [councils] as guarantors of the self-governance of the working class, he gives a very gloomy description of the *actual* German soviets [councils], personified by their congress of 1918:

Gentlemen, no revolutionary parliament in history has shown such
a timid, narrow, pedestrian spirit as the parliament of the revolution
assembled here.

Where are the great, uplifting, spiritual ideals that dominated the
French National Convention? Where is the youthful enthusiasm of
March 1848? Not a trace of either can be seen today.

And it is precisely when Däumig discovers the "timid, narrow, pedestrian" spirit that dominates the German soviets [councils], that he
seeks the key to all the problems raised by the social revolution in the
slogan "All power to the soviets!"[23] All power to the timid, narrow, and
pedestrian as a means of skipping the pedestrian character of universal
suffrage! A strange paradox! But this paradox makes perfect sense, if in
the "subconscious" sphere the process is already taking place that, when
it passes into the sphere of consciousness, will find its expression in P.
Orlovskii's formula: "With the aid of the soviet system, state power
passes into the hands of the Communists." In other words, through
the intermediary of the soviets, the revolutionary minority *subjugates*
the "pedestrian" majority.

Note that Däumig is in fact right. In the first all-German Congress of Soviets [the First German Congress of Workers' and Soldiers'
Councils], Scheidemann's partisans and the soldiers held an over-
whelming majority. The congress, you might say, smelled of timidity
and pedestrianism. Four and a half years of "class collaboration" and "the
brotherhood of the trenches" had not failed to leave their mark both
on the worker in overalls and the worker in a grey military overcoat.

Similarly, our Bolsheviks were right when, in June 1917, they
shrugged their shoulders in indignation at the hopelessly timid spirit
that dominated the First All-Russian Congress of Soviets, despite the
fact that it—unlike its German counterpart—was headed by a politician like I. G. Tsereteli, an individual who had an outstanding ability
to raise the masses above their everyday timidity.[24] We, the [Menshe-
vik] Internationalists, who had the pleasure of being in the minority at
this congress, also despaired at the timidity and lack of understanding
shown again and again by the immense "swamp" of the Menshevik and

Social Revolutionary majority in the face of great world events and the most complex socio-political problems. And, we could not understand why the Bolsheviks sitting to the left of us—who were even more indignant at the spirit [dominating the congress]—nonetheless called for "All power to the soviets!" We could not understand them when, during this congress, they organized a demonstration with the object of forcing such an assembly to take all power into its own hands.

As was mentioned above, fear of the triumph by "the timid majority" prompted even Lenin, after 3 July 1917, to propose removing from the agenda the slogan "All power to the soviets!," recognizing this old slogan as being outdated, and replacing it with "All power to the Bolsheviks!"[25] We might perhaps find a German parallel to this in the Spartacist decision to *boycott* the election to the second (April) all-German Congress of Councils [Soviets].

The subsequent course of the Russian Revolution cured Lenin of his temporary lack of faith. The soviets fulfilled their intended role. A wave of spontaneous bourgeois-revolutionary enthusiasm swept through the broad masses of workers and peasants, dissolving their "timid, narrow, and pedestrian" spirit (along with something else). On the crest of this wave, the Communists seized the machinery of power. Then the role of the rebellious self-active [*samodeiatel'ni*] element was played out. The servant had done its work. [The servant could now go and leave the stage.][26] The state which had been constructed with the aid of the "power of the soviets" became the "Soviet Power." The Communist minority organized into this state insulated itself, once and for all, against any new recurrence of the "narrow" and "pedestrian" sentiments in the masses. The idea that had glimmered in the sphere of the subconscious could finally be brought to fruition in the theory of P. Orlovskii, sanctioned by the practice of the Kashin Communists.

Dictatorship as a means of *protecting the people from their innate reactionary "pedestrianism"*—such was the historical origin of revolutionary communism at the time when the proletariat began to see through the lies and hypocrisy of the liberty proclaimed by capitalism.

Buonarotti, the theoretician of Babeuf's communist conspiracy of 1796, concluded that as soon as power was taken over by the communists, they would need to isolate France by an impassable barrier in order to shield the masses from pernicious influences coming from other countries. He demanded that no publication should appear in France without the authorization of the communist government.[27] According to Wilhelm Weitling, writing in the 1840s:

> All Socialists, with the exception of the followers of Fourier . . . are agreed that the form of government which is called the rule of the people is totally unsuitable, and even dangerous, for the young principle of social organization about to be realized.[28]

Étienne Cabet wrote that in each city in a socialist society, there could be only a *single* newspaper, which would of course be issued by the government.[29] The people were to be protected from the temptation of seeking the truth in the clash of opposing opinions.

At the political trial arising from the 1839 insurrection led by Blanqui and Barbes, a communist catechism was found in the possession of the accused. This catechism dealt, among other things, with the problem of dictatorship:

> Unquestionably, after a revolution carried out in the spirit of our ideas, it will be necessary to create a dictatorial power whose mission is to lead the revolutionary movement. This dictatorial power will necessarily draw its strength from the assent of the armed population, which, acting for the common good and for humanitarian progress, will obviously represent the enlightened will of the great majority of the nation. . . .
>
> In order to be strong, to be able to act quickly, dictatorial power will have to be concentrated in as few men as possible. . . .
>
> To undermine the old society, to destroy it to its very foundations, to overthrow the internal and external enemies of the Republic, to prepare the new foundations of social organization, and, finally, to lead the people from the revolutionary government to a regular republican government—such are the responsibilities of the dictatorial power and the limits of its duration.[30]

The question is: How great is the theoretical distance separating those that stand for "Soviet Power," in the manner of P. Orlovskii and the Kashin Communists, from the Parisian communists of 1839?

9. Metaphysical Materialism and Dialectical Materialism

The working class is the product of capitalist society. As such, its mindset is subjected to the influence of this society. Its consciousness is developed under the pressure of its bourgeois masters. School and church, the barracks and the factory, the press and social life—in short, all the factors shaping the consciousness of the proletarian masses—are powerful conductors of the influence of bourgeois ideas and attitudes. That is fairly obvious. As Charles Naine pointed out in the lines cited above, for revolutionary socialists, at least in Switzerland, precisely the observation of these facts served as the starting point for their belief in the necessity of a dictatorship by a minority of conscious proletarians over all the people, and even over the majority of the proletariat itself.

Emile Pouget, the prominent syndicalist leader, wrote:

> Were the democratic mechanism to be applied in workers' organizations, the indifference of the unconscious and non-unionized majority would paralyze any action. But the minority is not inclined to abdicate its claims and aspirations before the inertia of a mass not yet energized and enlivened by the spirit of revolt.
>
> Therefore, for the conscious minority, there is an obligation to act without taking into account the sluggish mass. . . .
>
> The amorphous mass, numerous and compact though it may be, has little cause to complain about this. It is the first to benefit from the action of the minority. . . .
>
> Who would blame the minority for its selfless initiative? Certainly not those lacking consciousness, whom the militants consider to be little more than human zeros, which only acquire numerical value when another number is placed to their left.

This is the enormous difference in method distinguishing syndicalism from democratism. The latter, through the mechanism of universal suffrage, gives leadership to the unconscious, the laggards ... and stifles the minorities who carry within them the future. The syndicalist method gives diametrically opposite results: the impetus for the movement comes from the conscious, the rebels. All those of good will are called on to act, to participate in the movement.[31]

The thesis about the inevitable mental/spiritual subjugation of the proletarian masses by the capitalist class also forms one of the premises of P. Orlovskii's conclusions, given in the preceding chapter.

This thesis is undoubtedly *materialist* in nature. It is based on the recognition of the dependence of people's thinking on their material environment.

Such a recognition was characteristic of many socialists and communists, utopian and revolutionary, in the late eighteenth and early nineteenth centuries.

We can discover its traces in Robert Owen, Cabet, Weitling, and Blanqui.[32] They all recognized that the mental servitude of the masses was generated by the material conditions of their situation in the present society. And all of them drew the conclusion that only a fundamental change in the material conditions in which the masses lived, only a fundamental transformation of society, would render the masses capable of directing their own destiny.

But who will change these conditions?

The wise educators of humanity who come out of the privileged classes, that is to say, individuals freed from the material conditions that overwhelm the thinking of the masses—that was the answer of the social utopians.

A revolutionary minority composed of individuals who, for more or less accidental reasons, have shielded their mind and wills from this pressure, persons who in our society represent an exception that proves the rule—this, as we have seen, was the answer of revolutionary communists like Weitling and Blanqui, and the conception of their epigones of the anarcho-syndicalist type, like Pouget and Gustave Hervé of blessed memory.[33]

For some, it was a benevolent dictatorship; for others, a violent one that was to be the *deus ex machina*, the external factor that was going to bridge the gap between the social situation that produced the spiritual bondage of the masses and the social situation that would make possible their full development as human beings.

"The character of human beings," wrote Robert Owen, "is formed by environment and education.... From this follows the task: to transform these two factors shaping character in such a manner that human beings become virtuous."[34]

According to Owen, the task of performing this transformation fell to the legislators, to the philanthropists, to the pedagogues.

It is easy to see that both pacifist and revolutionary utopians were only *half* materialist. They understood in a purely metaphysical way the thesis about human psychology's dependence on the material environment. That is, [they understood it] *statically*, being unaware of the *dynamics* of the social process. Their materialism was not *dialectical*. The relationship between a given state of social consciousness and the conditioned state of social being, which determines the former, were understood by them [the utopians] as something frozen, once and for all given. They, therefore, stopped being materialists and became pure idealists as soon as they tried to solve the practical problem of how to change the social environment in order to make possible a change in the condition of the masses.

Marx long ago observed in his "Theses on Feuerbach":

> The materialist doctrine that people are products of circumstances
> and education, and that, therefore, changed people are products of
> other circumstances and changed education, forgets that it is the
> people who change the circumstances and that the educators must
> themselves be educated. Hence, this doctrine must of necessity
> divide society into two parts, one of which is elevated *above* the other
> (in Robert Owen, for example).[35]

Applied to the class struggle of the proletariat, this means the following. Driven by the very "circumstances" of capitalist society that form its character as a subjugated class, the proletariat enters into a struggle against the society that subjugates it. The process of this struggle modifies the social "circumstances." It modifies the environment in which the working class lives. In this way, the working class modifies its own character. From a class reflecting passively the mental servitude to which it is subjected, it becomes a class that actively overthrows all subjugation, including that of the mind.

This process is far from straightforward. It does not take place evenly in all strata of the proletariat, nor all aspects of proletarian consciousness. It will not, of course, be complete when a combination of historical circumstances makes possible or even inevitable the working class tearing the apparatus of political power from the hands of the bourgeoisie. The workers are condemned to enter the realm of socialism burdened by a significant share of those "vices of the oppressed," the yoke that Ferdinand Lassalle had so eloquently urged them to throw off.[36]

In the process of the struggle against capitalism, the proletariat modifies the material environment surrounding it, thereby modifying its own character and emancipating itself intellectually/spiritually. Likewise, in the process of using its conquered power to systematically construct the entire social order, the proletariat eventually frees itself completely from the intellectual influence of the old society, because it achieves a radical transformation in the material environment by which its character is determined.

But only "eventually!" Only as the result of a long, painful and contradictory process in which, as in all preceding historical processes, social creativity develops only under the hammer of iron necessity, under the imperious pressure of elementary needs.

The conscious will of the advanced members of the class can appreciably shorten and facilitate this process. It can never *bypass* it.

Some people assume that if a compact revolutionary minority, having the willpower to establish socialism, seizes the machinery of state administration and concentrates in its own hands all the means of production and distribution as well as all organizational apparatuses of the masses and all sources of education,[37] it may—guided by the ideals of communism—create conditions in which the popular mind will, little by little, be purged of its old intellectual heritage and be filled with a new content. Then, and only then, will the people be able to stand on their own and walk the path of socialism.

If this utopia could be fully implemented, it would lead to the diametrically opposite result, if only because, in Marx's words, the "educators must be educated," and because, therefore, *such* a dictatorship, and the relations established between the dictatorial minority and the mass, educate the dictators in all possible ways, but not as people capable of directing the course of social development along the path of building a new society. It goes without saying that such an education can only corrupt and spiritually debase *the masses*.

The only possible builder of the new society, and consequently the only possible successor to the former dominant classes in the administration of the state, is the proletarian *class* considered as a whole—and we are using the word in its broadest sense, including knowledge workers, the workers of intellectual labour, whose co-operation in the direction of the state and the administration of the economy is so obviously necessary. The proletarians will also find it indispensable to win the active support or at least the friendly neutrality of very broad layers within the non-proletarian producers of the city and countryside. This follows from the very nature of the social revolution, the realization of which is the proletariat's historic mission. This change must manifest itself in every part of the life of society. Only if it generates the maximum moral and spiritual energy will the proletariat be able to take in its hands the vast heritage of capitalism without squandering it and put into motion capitalism's gigantic forces of production so that the result is real social equality based on an increase in the general well-being. This is only possible with the maximum development of the organized *self-activity* [*samodeiatel'nost*] of all the component parts of the working class—that is, under conditions that absolutely preclude the dictatorship of a minority standing "above society," along with the indispensable companions of such a dictatorship: terror and bureaucracy.

In the process of freely constructing a new society, the proletariat will re-educate itself and eliminate from its character those traits that come directly into conflict with the great tasks it faces. This applies both to the working class as a whole and to each of its individual strata. Naturally, the duration of this process will vary for each of these strata. Socialist policy, standing on the firm ground of historical reality must reckon with this fact—the inevitably slow, sometimes very slow, pace of the developmental process by which the psychological adaptation of the whole class to its new situation will be accomplished. Any attempt to artificially force the pace of this process is certain to yield the opposite result. For the goal to be achieved, a whole series of historically imposed compromises will be found absolutely indispensable, in order to adapt to the intellectual/spiritual level attained by the different strata within the working class at the moment of capitalism's collapse.

But the ultimate goal justifies only those compromises that do not contradict it, that do not bar the road to its realization. Consequently, it is inadvisable to make too far-reaching a compromise with either the destructive elements that attract some sections of the working class or with the conservative inertia of other sections of the working class.

A compromise made with a hostile class is nearly always fatal to the revolution. A compromise that guarantees the unity of the class in its struggle against the enemy and makes possible the self-active [*samodeiatel'ni*] participation of the broadest masses of this class in the work of the revolutionary government can only move the revolution forward.

To be sure, this will be at the cost of a longer, more winding path of development for the revolution, compared to the straight line that could be drawn under the conditions of a minority dictatorship. But here, as in mechanics, "what is lost in distance is made up in speed," the speed in more rapidly overcoming the inner psychological obstacles that arise in the way of the revolutionary class and hamper it in its attempt to achieve its aims. By contrast, the straight line, preferred by the doctrinaires of the violent revolution because it is shorter, leads in practice to the maximum of psychological resistance, and because of this, to the minimum productivity from creative social revolutionary work.

III.

Decomposition or Conquest of the State?

10. Marx and the State

The supporters of a "pure soviet system" (an expression common in Germany) do not realize, as a rule, that the political constructs of contemporary Bolshevism are essentially about the organization of a minority dictatorship. On the contrary, the supporters of a "pure soviet system" begin by sincerely looking around for political forms that might best express the genuine will of the majority. They come to "sovietism" only after rejecting the democracy of universal suffrage—precisely because it does not express this. While the *psychology* of the extreme leftists in their passion for "sovietism" is characterized by the desire to jump over the historical inertia of the masses, of the majority of the people, dominating their *logic* is the idea of a new political form, "at last discovered," that best expresses the class rule of the proletariat, just as the democratic republic best expresses the class domination of the bourgeoisie.

The idea that the realization of workers' power requires the use of social forms that are absolutely and fundamentally different from those in which the power of the bourgeoisie is manifested has existed since the dawn of the *revolutionary* labour movement. We find it, for example, in the vigorous propaganda of the immediate predecessors of the Chartist movement: the construction worker James Morrison and his friend, the writer James Smith.[1] While the advanced workers of the period were only beginning to feel the need to win political power and for this purpose to achieve universal suffrage, Smith wrote in his journal *The Crisis* on 12 April 1834:

> The only House of Commons is a House of Trades [unions]. . . . We shall have a new set of boroughs when the unions are organized: every trade [union] shall be a borough, and every trade [union] shall have a council of representatives to conduct its affairs. Our present commoners know nothing of the interests of the people, and care not for them. . . . The character of the Reformed Parliament is now blasted [discredited], and . . . is not easily recovered. It will be replaced with a House of Trades.[2]

In the same period, Morrison wrote in his publication *The Pioneer*, 31 May 1834:

> The growing power and growing intelligence of trades unions . . . will become, by its own self-acquired importance, a most influential, we might almost say *dictatorial*, part of the body politic. When this happens we have gained all that we want: we have gained universal suffrage, for if every member of the Union be a constituent, and the Union itself becoming a *vital member* of the State, it instantly erects itself into a House of Trades which must supply the place of the present House of Commons, and direct the industrial affairs of the country, according to the will of the trades. . . . With us, universal suffrage will begin in our lodges, extend to the general union, *embrace the management of trade, and finally swallow up the political power.*[3]

Substitute "soviet" for "union," "ispolkom" [executive committee] for "council of representatives," "Soviet Congress" for "House of Trades," and you have an outline of the "soviet system" established on the basis of productive units.

Polemicizing with these representatives of the *syndicalist* conception of the dictatorship of the proletariat, Bronterre O'Brien, who later headed the Chartists, wrote in his newspaper *Poor Man's Guardian*: "Universal suffrage does not signify meddling with politics, but the rule of the people in the state and municipality, *a Government therefore in favour of the working man.*"[4]

Drawing heavily on the experience of the revolutionary workers' movement in England, the 1848 communism (scientific socialism) of Marx and Engels, identified the problem of winning state power by the proletariat with the problem of organizing a consistent democracy.

The Communist Manifesto declared: "The first step in the revolution by the working class is to raise the proletariat to the position of ruling class, to win the battle of democracy."[5]

According to Lenin, the *Manifesto* poses the question of the state "in an extremely abstract manner, in the most general terms and expressions."[6] The problem of the conquest of state power begins to be presented more concretely in the *Eighteenth Brumaire*. Its refinement is completed in *The Civil War in France*, written on the basis of the experience of the Paris Commune. Lenin believes that, in the course of this refinement, Marx's understanding of the dictatorship of the proletariat, which today forms the basis of Bolshevism, was fully defined.

In 1852, in the *Eighteenth Brumaire*, Marx wrote: "All [previous] revolutions perfected this [state] machine instead of breaking it."[7]

On 12 April 1871, in a letter to Kugelmann, he formulated his viewpoint on the problem of revolution as follows:

> If you look at the last chapter of my *Eighteenth Brumaire*, you will find that I say that the next attempt of the French revolution will be no longer, as before, to transfer the bureaucratic military machine from one hand to another, but to *break* it, and that is essential for every real people's revolution on the Continent. And this is what our heroic Party comrades in Paris are attempting.[8]

In this sense, Marx declared (in *The Civil War in France*) that the Commune was "a Republic that was not only to supersede the monarchical form of class-rule, but class-rule itself."[9]

What, then, was the Commune? It was an attempt to bring about a truly and consistently democratic state by destroying the old military-bureaucratic state apparatus. It was an attempt to establish a state based entirely on the sovereignty of the people [*narodovlastie*]. Marx speaks of the eradication of the bureaucracy, the police, and the standing army, he speaks of the election and recall of all officials, of the broadest local self-government, of the concentration of all power in the hands of the people's representatives (thus doing away with the gap between the legislative and executive branches of the government, and replacing the "talking" parliament with a "working institution").[10] To this point, then, in his defence of the Commune, Marx remains faithful to the conception of social revolution presented in *The Communist Manifesto*, in which the dictatorship of the proletariat is identified with winning "the battle of democracy."[11] He therefore remains quite consistent when, in his letter to Kugelmann, quoted above, he stresses that "for every true people's revolution *on the Continent*" (our emphasis, Martov), it is essential to break "the bureaucratic military machine."[12]

It is interesting to compare the conclusions on this question drawn by Marx and Engels from their experiences in the events of 1848 with the conclusions drawn by Herzen. In his *Letters from France and Italy*, Herzen wrote:

> Universal suffrage, when combined with the monarchical organization of the state, the absurd division of powers, of which the adherents of constitutional forms so boasted, the religious concept of representation, and the police centralization of the entire state in the hands of the ministry, is as much an optical illusion as the equality that Christianity preached. The issue is by no means whether you gather once a year to elect a deputy and again return to the passive role of the governed. The entire social hierarchy had to be based on elections, the commune had to be allowed to elect its own government, and the department its own; all the proconsuls who receive their holy office from ministerial anointment had to be abolished;

only then would it be possible for the people to really make use of their rights and, moreover, to elect their central deputies efficiently.

On the contrary, the bourgeois republicans "wished to leave the cities and communes in the most complete dependence on the executive power and applied the democratic idea of universal suffrage to a single civic act."[13]

Like Marx, Herzen denounced the supposedly-democratic bourgeois republic in the name of a republic that was genuinely and consistently democratic. And like Herzen, Marx attacked universal suffrage as a deceptive decoration attached to the "monarchic organization of the state," bequeathed by the past. [Instead, he favoured] a state system built from top to bottom on universal suffrage and the sovereignty of the people.

Commenting on Marx's idea, Lenin rightfully observes:

> This was understandable in 1871, when England was still the model of a purely capitalist country, but without militarism and, to a considerable degree, without bureaucracy. Marx therefore excluded England, where a revolution, even a people's revolution, then seemed possible, and indeed was possible, without [the prior condition] of first destroying the "ready-made state machinery."[14]

Unfortunately, Lenin hurried on without giving much thought to all the questions that arise from this limitation posited by Marx.

That limitation, according to Lenin, allowed for a situation where the people's revolution would not need to destroy the ready-made state machinery; [the people's revolution] could make use of the ready-made state machinery if the latter did not have the military-bureaucratic character typical of the Continent. It was a question of an exception to the overall process of development, within the framework of and in spite of capitalism—the development in a country of *a democratic apparatus of self-governance*, which the military-bureaucratic machine had not succeeded in suppressing. In that case, according to Marx, the people's revolution had only to take possession of this apparatus and develop it in order to create a state form suitable for the realization of its creative tasks.

There was a reason that both Marx and Engels theorized the possibility that a socialist overturn in England could be brought about by *peaceful* means. This theoretical possibility rested precisely on the democratic character, capable of further development, of the English state system of their day.

Much water has flowed under the bridge since then. In both England and the United States, imperialism has created that "military-bureaucratic state machine" whose absence had constituted the main feature differentiating the political evolution of the Anglo-Saxon countries from the general type of capitalist states. At the present time, it is doubtful whether this distinctive feature [the absence of a military-bureaucratic state machine] will be preserved even in the younger Anglo-Saxon republics: Australia and New Zealand. "Today," Lenin correctly remarks, "in England and America, 'the precondition for any real people's revolution' is the *demolition*, the *destruction* of the 'ready-made state machinery.'"[15]

The theoretical possibility was not in the end realized. But the very fact that he admitted such a possibility shows us clearly Marx's true views, leaving no room for any arbitrary interpretation. What Marx called the "demolition of the ready-made state machine" in the *Eighteenth Brumaire* and in his letter to Kugelmann was the *destruction of the military-bureaucratic machine* that the bourgeois democratic system had inherited from the monarchy and developed in the process of establishing the domination of the bourgeois class. There is nothing in Marx's reasoning that even suggests *the destruction of the state organization as such* and the replacement of the state during the revolutionary period—that is, during the dictatorship of the proletariat—with some other social bond formed on a principle *opposed to that of the state*. Marx and Engels foresaw such a replacement only at the end of a prolonged process involving the "*withering away*" of the state,[16] the withering away of all the functions of social *coercion*, the result of the prolonged existence of a socialist society.

No wonder that Engels wrote in 1891, in his introduction to *The Civil War in France*:

> The state is ... an evil inherited by the proletariat after its victorious struggle for class supremacy, whose *worst sides* (our emphasis, Martov) the victorious proletariat, just like the Commune, cannot avoid having to lop off at once ... until such time as a generation reared in new, free social conditions, is able to throw the entire lumber of the state on the scrap-heap.[17]

This seems quite clear. The proletariat lops off "the worst sides" of the democratic state (for example, the police, the standing army, the self-perpetuating bureaucracy, excessive centralization, etc., etc.). But it does not eliminate the democratic state itself. On the contrary, it shapes and develops it [the democratic state] in order to have it replace the "ready-made military-bureaucratic machine," which must be smashed.

> If one thing is certain, it is that our party and the working class can only come to power under the form of a democratic republic. *This is even the specific form for the dictatorship of the proletariat, as the Great French Revolution has already shown.*[18]

So wrote Engels in his critique of the draft of the Erfurt program in 1891.[19] He does not speak of a "soviet" republic (this social form was as yet unknown), nor of a communist republic opposed to the state. Neither does he speak of a "trade-union republic" as conceived by Smith and Morrison or the French syndicalists. Explicitly and definitively, Engels speaks of a democratic republic—that is, of a state ("an evil inherited by the proletariat") democratized from top to bottom.

This is so explicit, so definitive, that when Lenin quotes these words, he finds it necessary to immediately obscure their meaning. "Engels," he says,

> reiterates here in a particularly striking form the fundamental idea that runs through all of Marx's works—namely, that it is the democratic republic that comes *closest to* the dictatorship of the proletariat (our emphasis, Martov). For such a republic—without in the

least eliminating the rule of capital, and, consequently, the oppression of the masses and the class struggle—inevitably leads to such an extension, development, expansion, and escalation of this struggle that, as soon as it becomes possible to satisfy the basic interests of the oppressed masses, this possibility is realized inevitably and solely through the dictatorship of the proletariat, through the leadership of those masses by the proletariat.[20]

Engels is not speaking about a political form that "comes closest to the dictatorship," as Lenin suggests in his comments, but rather about a "specific" political form in which *to implement* the dictatorship. According to Engels, the dictatorship is realized in a *democratic republic*.[21] Lenin sees the democratic republic merely as an arena in which to sharpen the class struggle to the extreme, thus confronting the proletariat with the task of dictatorship. For Lenin, then, since the democratic republic finds its conclusion in the dictatorship of the proletariat, the former, having given birth to the latter, so to speak, naturally dies in the very act of its birth. Engels, on the contrary, believes that by gaining supremacy in the democratic republic and thus realizing its dictatorship within it, the proletariat is thereby, for the first time, investing the democratic republic with a character that is genuinely, fundamentally, and completely democratic. That is why, in 1848, Engels and Marx equated the notion of raising "the proletariat to the position of ruling class" with that of winning "the battle of democracy." That is why in *The Civil War*, Marx emphasized, in the experience of the Commune, the absolute triumph of the principles of sovereignty of the people [*narodovlastie*]: universal franchise, election, and recall of all officials. That is why in 1891, in his preface to *The Civil War*, Engels once again wrote:

> Against this transformation of the state and the organs of the state from servants of society into masters of society—an inevitable transformation in all previous states—the Commune made use of two infallible means. In the first place, it filled all posts—administrative, judicial and educational—by election on the basis of universal suffrage of all concerned, subject to the right of recall at any time by

the same electors. And, in the second place, all officials, high or low, were paid only the wages received by other workers.[22]

Universal suffrage is therefore an "infallible means" by which to prevent the transformation of the state [and the organs of the state] "from servants of society into masters of society." Thus, the state *conquered* by the proletariat in the form of a consistently democratic republic can be a real "servant of society."

Is it not obvious that when Engels speaks this way and identifies, at the same time, a democratic republic of *this kind* with the *dictatorship of the proletariat*, he is not employing the latter term to indicate *a form of government* but to denote *the social character* of state power? This was exactly what Kautsky emphasized in his *Dictatorship of the Proletariat* when he says that for Marx such a dictatorship was not a question "of a form of government but of a condition which must everywhere arise when the proletariat has conquered political power."[23] Any other interpretation leads inexorably to a glaring contradiction between Marx's statement that the Paris Commune was the embodiment of the dictatorship of the proletariat and his reference to the consistent democracy implemented by the Paris Commune.

The above quotation from Lenin demonstrates that—in his rare moments of spiritual communion with the first teachers of scientific socialism—even he was able to rise above a simplistic conception of class dictatorship, its reduction to *dictatorial forms of organization* of power, and understand it precisely as a distinct "political condition." In the above quotation from *The State and Revolution*, Lenin equates the "dictatorship of the proletariat" with the "leadership of those (popular) masses by the proletariat." This equation is entirely in the spirit of Marx and Engels. It is the way that Marx depicted the dictatorship of the proletariat during the Paris Commune when he wrote "this was the first revolution in which the working class was openly acknowledged as the only class [still] capable of social initiative, [acknowledged] even by the great bulk of the Paris middle class—shopkeepers, tradesmen, merchants—the wealthy capitalists alone excepted."[24]

It is the voluntary acceptance by the masses of the population of the leadership of the working class in the struggle against capitalism, that is the essential condition for the "political status" that is called the "dictatorship of the proletariat." Similarly, it is the voluntary acceptance by the broad popular masses of the leadership of the bourgeoisie that makes it possible to call the political conditions existing in France, England, and the United States the "dictatorship of the bourgeoisie." This dictatorship in no way disappears when the bourgeoisie considers it feasible, by granting them universal suffrage, to offer formal sovereignty to the peasants and the petite bourgeoisie under its leadership. Similarly, the dictatorship of the proletariat about which Marx and Engels spoke is also realizable on the basis of the same sovereignty of the people and the wide application of universal suffrage.[25]

Therefore, if we keep in mind the assessments by Marx and Engels, cited previously, concerning dictatorship, the democratic republic, and the state as "an evil [inherited by the proletariat]," we cannot but arrive at the conclusion that, for Marx and Engels, the problem of the conquest of political power by the proletariat was reduced to the destruction of the bureaucratic-military machine, which commands the bourgeois state in spite of its democratic parliamentarism, and to the development of a new state machine based on the consistent implementation of democracy, universal suffrage, and the broadest self-governance, under the condition that the proletariat actually leads the majority of the people.

In that regard, Marx and Engels continue and extend the political tradition of the Montagnards of 1793 and the Chartists of the O'Brien school.[26]

There is no doubt that it is possible to discover in the works of Marx and Engels traces of a different set of ideas. These appear to offer grounds for the thesis that the *forms and institutions* in which the political power of the proletariat manifests itself take on a fundamentally new character, fundamentally opposed to the forms and institutions that embody the political power of the bourgeoisie, fundamentally opposed to *the state* as such. Consideration of these traces of an entirely different set of ideas merits a separate chapter.

11. The Commune of 1871

When Marx was writing about the Commune, not only did he have to present his views on the dictatorship of the proletariat, simultaneously and above all else he had to defend the Commune against its numerous embittered enemies. This circumstance could not fail to influence the very assessment of the slogans and forms of the movement.

The revolutionary explosion that led to the seizure of Paris by the armed proletariat on 18 March 1871—on the basis of an acute struggle between labour and capital—was affected by the clash between the democratic-republican population of the French capital and the conservative masses of the provinces, especially the rural masses.

During the preceding two decades, the "backward peasantry" of France had suppressed revolutionary and republican Paris by supporting [the Second Empire's] extreme bureaucratic centralism. As a result, the uprising of the Parisian democracy against the representatives of those backward peasants gathered at Versailles took on the character of a struggle for *municipal autonomy*.[27]

At first, this character of the movement gained the Commune the sympathy of many representatives of a purely bourgeois radicalism—supporters of administrative decentralization and broad local self-government. But this aspect of the Paris Commune of 1871 also obscured—even from the leaders of the Commune—the true nature and historic meaning of the movement they were leading.

In his memoir about the [First] International, the famous anarchist James Guillaume tells how immediately after the outbreak of the revolt, the Jura Federation, which he headed, sent its delegate Jacquault to Paris in order to learn the best way to help the movement—a movement the Jurassians saw as the beginning of a worldwide social revolution. They were very surprised when their delegate returned with a report that E. Varlin, the most prominent leader of the left-wing French Internationalists, responded to this question with an expression of astonishment. According to Varlin, the revolution of 18 March had only one, purely local aim—the conquest of municipal freedoms for Paris. According to Varlin, the conquest of these freedoms was not expected to have any social and revolutionary consequences for the rest of Europe.[28]

This, of course, could have been said only during the first days of the Commune. Soon, the historic meaning of their revolution began to reveal itself to the Paris proletariat. Nevertheless, when it came to conceiving of the Commune's aims, the influence of narrow bourgeois ideas of municipal autonomy continued to be felt until the very end. It was not without reason that Marx in his *Civil War* had to refute British liberals and even Bismarck himself, who tried to depict the whole Commune movement as aimed at achieving municipal autonomy.

And was it not this lack of clarity in the Communards' *ideology* that Marx had in mind later, in one of his letters to Kugelmann, reporting on the rebellion against him by the exiled leaders of the Commune in London? Marx reminded the activists of the Commune that it was he who had "defended the honour" of the 1871 revolution.[29] Marx defended the Commune precisely by revealing the historic meaning of its heroic deeds, a meaning that had escaped the consciousness of even the Communard combatants.

But besides bourgeois radicalism, other ideological influences were also strong—anarchist Proudhonism and Hébertian Blanquism.[30] These two tendencies are organically intertwined with the general French working-class movement. For the representatives of both these ideological currents, the slogan "the commune" carried a meaning diametrically opposed to that assigned to it by bourgeois-democratic decentralist radicalism. These opposing views were united only in a purely formal sense, the fact that each took a stand against the bureaucratic and centralizing leanings of the state apparatus bequeathed by the Second Empire.

In the second half of the 1860s, French Blanquism, having drawn closer to the working class masses, partially overcame the narrow conspiratorial and bourgeois-Jacobin character of the political tradition under whose influence they (and along with them, the Babeuf school) had grown up. While Blanqui continued to draw his political inspiration from the heritage of the eighteenth-century revolution, he and the most active of his followers became more critical of the Jacobin forms of popular sovereignty [*narodovlastie*] and revolutionary dictatorship. They tried to find ideological support for the proletarian movement of their time in the revolutionary tradition of the so-called Hébertists— the extreme left-wing of the sans-culottes of the French Revolution.

In 1793–94, Hébert and his supporters relied on the true "common poor"[31] of the Parisian *faubourgs*, whose vague social and revolutionary hopes they expressed. By means of this support, the Hébertists turned the Paris Commune into an instrument by which they might exert pressure on the central government. Relying directly on the armed masses, they sought to transform the Paris Commune of 1794 into the centre of all revolutionary power. Until Robespierre reduced it to the level of a subordinate administrative mechanism (which he accomplished by crushing the Hébertists and sending their leaders to the guillotine), the Commune of 1794, being in fact an elected body of the active revolutionary elements among the Parisian urban poor, embodied the instinctive desire of these urban poor to impose their dictatorship on politically backward rural and provincial France.[32]

The Commune as the centre of the revolutionary will and the direct revolutionary creativity of the proletarian masses—contrasted with the democratic state—that became the fighting political slogan of the young Blanquists toward the end of the Second Empire.[33]

Alongside this "Hébertist" current and intertwined with it—in the course of the revolution of 18 March—another political current manifested itself: anarcho-Proudhonism.

For this latter current, just as for the Hébertist-Blanquist one, the "commune" was a lever for a revolutionary overturn. But it was not the commune as a political organization with a specifically revolutionary character, opposed to another political organization—a more or less democratic state—that was to obtain the effective submission of the latter by means of the dictatorship of Paris over France. The "commune" they had in mind was a "natural" *social* organization of producers. They opposed every state as an "artificial" (that is, political) union of citizens established on the basis of hierarchical subordination through the "fraudulent" apparatus of popular representation. Understood this way, the commune was not to rise above the state or subordinate it to its dictatorship. It was to *separate* itself from the state and invite all the 36,000 communes (cities and villages) of France to do the same, with the purpose of decomposing the state and replacing it with a free federation of communes.

"What does Paris want?" asked *La Commune* on 19 April, answering its own question as follows:

> The absolute autonomy of the Commune extended to all localities in France, assuring to each one its full rights, to every Frenchman the full exercise of his faculties and abilities as a man, citizen, and worker.
>
> The autonomy of the Commune will be limited only by the right to equal autonomy of all the other municipalities adhering to the pact. Such an association of communes will assure French unity.[34]

From this evolved a consistently *federalist* program in the Proudhonist-Bakuninist sense, which recognized a voluntary pact as the only tie between individual communities and which ruled out any complex apparatus of general state administration. The "Federalists" were particularly eager to be called "Communards.

"On the 18th of March," wrote the Bakuninist Arthur Arnould, a member of the Commune, "the people declared that it was necessary to escape the vicious circle, to cut off the evil at its root—not merely to change masters, but to cease having masters altogether. With an admirable insight into the truth, to achieve this goal they [the people] proclaimed the means that could lead to it—*the autonomy of the Commune and a federation of communes.*

> It was a matter of elucidating, *for the first time*, the actual rules, the just and normal laws, which can assure the real independence of the individual and the group, whether communal or corporative, and then to link similar groups together, so that they would enjoy at the same time, the *union* that creates strength . . . and the *autonomy* that

is essential to ... the unlimited expansion of all original capacities, all productive and progressive characteristics.[35]

This communal federalism was presented by the anarcho-Proudhonists as the [model for an] organization in which the economic relations of the producers could be *directly* expressed.

"It is up to each autonomous grouping," says the same Arnould, "whether communal or corporative, depending on circumstances within its own circle, to solve the social question, that is, those questions related to *the property question, the relation between labour and capital* ... etc."[36]

Note the caveat: "communal or corporative, depending on circumstances ..." The viewpoint of the Federalist-Communard approaches quite closely the outlook that led successively to: in 1833 the Morrison and Smith formula of a "house of trade-unions"; at the beginning of the twentieth century, the doctrine of Georges Sorel, Édouard Berth and [Daniel] De Leon, on the replacement of the "artificial" subdivisions of the modern state by a federation of "natural" corporative (occupational) cells; and in 1917–19, the conception of the "soviet system."[37] The "communal grouping," comments Arnould in a footnote, "corresponds to ancient *political* organization" while "the corporative grouping would have corresponded to the *social* organization."[38] Thus the communal organization was to serve as a *transition* from the state to a "corporative" federation.

This opposition of a "political" organization to a "social" organization suggests that the "breaking up of the state machinery" by the proletariat will immediately restore "natural" relationships among the producers, relations that can only manifest themselves outside of political norms and institutions. This opposition is *the basis* of the social revolutionary tendencies among the Communards.

> All that the socialists call for, everything they would not be able to
> obtain without horrible convulsions, without bitter, painful, and
> ruinous struggles from a *strong and centralizing power*, no matter
> how democratic it is presumed to be, they will achieve in an orderly
> manner, with certainty and without violence, through the simple

activation of the communal principle of free groupings and federation.

The solution can belong only to the *corporative* and *productive*
groups, linked together federally, and freed therefore from governmental and administrative—*that is to say, political* (our emphasis,
Martov)—shackles, which till now have maintained, by oppression,
the antagonism between capital and labour, subjecting the latter to
the former.[39]

Such was the understanding of the essence and meaning of the
Commune by its *most advanced* militants, most directly linked with
the social revolutionary class movement of the French proletariat.

Charles Seignobos is certainly wrong when he writes (in his essay
on the Commune, found in the *Histoire générale* edited by Lavisse and
Rambaud) that the revolutionaries moved away from their initial aim—
the seizure of power in France—and instead moved to the cause of a
self-sustaining commune in Paris because they found themselves on the
defensive, isolated from the rest of France.[40] This circumstance merely
facilitated the triumph of the anarcho-federalist ideas in the Commune movement. If, in the program statements of the Communards,
the Hébertist conception of the Commune as dictator exercising power
over France, was superseded by the Proudhonist idea of an apolitical
federation, it was because *the class* character of the movement was
sharply outlined in the struggle between Paris and Versailles. At that
time, the class consciousness of the proletariat in the small industries of
Paris revolved entirely around the ideological opposition of a "natural"
union of producers within society to the "artificial" union of producers
within the state. We have already seen how Varlin gave the Commune,
in its early days, a purely democratic-radical interpretation. In its proclamation of 23 March 1871, the Paris section of the International wrote:
"The independence of the Commune is the guarantee of a contract
whose clauses, freely debated, will bring an end to class antagonism
and will assure social equality." That is, with the fall of the power of
coercion exercised by the state, it becomes possible to create a simple
"natural" social bond among the members of society—a bond based on

their economic interdependence. And it is precisely the Commune that is destined to become the framework within which this relationship can be organized.

"We have demanded the emancipation of the workers," continues the proclamation, "and the communal government guarantees it, for it shall furnish each citizen with the means of defending his rights and effectively controlling the acts of its representatives charged with managing its interests and determining the progressive application of social reforms."[41]

It is clear at a glance that, for the anarchist idea of *a workers' commune*—that is, a union of producers, as contrasted to a union of citizens within *the state*—the proclamation has discreetly substituted the idea of a *political* commune, the prototype of the modern state, a state microcosm within which the representation of interests and the satisfaction of social needs become specialized functions, just as (though in a simpler form) in the complex mechanism of the modern state. P. Lavrov understood this quite well. He notes in his book on the Commune:

> In the nineteenth century, the community of communal interests completely disappeared in the face of the rise of the internal struggle between classes. As a unified moral whole, the community *did not exist at all* [Lavrov's emphasis]. In each community, the irreconcilable camps of the proletariat and the big bourgeoisie confronted each other, with the struggle becoming more complicated due to the presence of the most diverse groups of the petite bourgeoisie. For a moment, Paris was united by a common *affect*: anger with *the Bordeaux* and Versailles Assemblies. But a transient affect cannot be the foundation of a political order.

The "real autonomous principle of the system," Lavrov writes in the same book, "to which the social revolution must lead is not a political commune that permits inequality, a mixture of parasitic and working classes, etc., but *a solidaristic grouping of workers of various kinds, rallied to the program of the social revolution*" (our emphasis, Martov).[42]

P. Lavrov speaks definitively of a "confusion of two notions."

On the one hand, the autonomous political commune, the ideal of the Middle Ages, in the struggle for which the bourgeoisie solidified itself and grew strong during the first phases of its development. On the other hand, the autonomous proletarian commune, which is to emerge after the economic victory of the proletariat over its enemies, after the establishment, within the community, of a social solidarity that is inconceivable as long as the economic exploitation of labour by capital continues, and therefore as long as class hatred within each community is inevitable. When we analyze the demands of communal autonomy as they were generally formulated in the course of the struggle in question, it may seem strange how the indisputably socialist militants of the Commune saw the connection between the fundamental question of socialism, about the struggle of labour against capital, and the slogan of the "free commune" that they inscribed on their banner.[43]

The strangeness of which Lavrov speaks lies in the fact that a social form into which, we believe, the more or less complete structure of a socialist economy will be moulded, is [simultaneously] assumed to be necessary for the very process of transforming the capitalist system into a socialist one. This is the same strangeness, the same contradiction, that can be observed among anarchists. It is an indisputable fact that once the foundations of the private economic order are destroyed and the entire national economy is transformed into a communal, socialist economy, the need for the state as an organization that rises above the producer disappears. The anarchists conclude from this that the *precondition* for this social transformation is "the demolition of the state," its "decomposition" into its simplest cells, into "communes." There existed in the ideology of the Communards a conflation of Proudhonist, Hébertist, and bourgeois-autonomist notions. As a result, in their discourse on the essence of the revolution, they switched quite easily from the political "commune"—a territorial unit created by the preceding bourgeois development and that, in essence, is the main part of *the state* mechanism—to the labour or "corporative" commune, a commune of freely associating workers that we can easily imagine as the probable form of the social grouping in a fully finished socialist system in which the collective work of perhaps one or two generations will have rendered possible the "gradual dying out of the state" as predicted by Engels.[44]

Dunoyer, one of the witnesses who appeared before the commission of inquiry appointed by the Versailles National Assembly after the fall of the Commune (quoted by Lavrov in his *Paris Commune*), gave interesting insights into the fact that the communalist ideas, as they were perceived by the workers, were nothing more than an attempt to transpose the forms of *their own* militant organization into the organization of society.

"The grouping of workers within the International by sections and federations of sections was one of the elements in the development of the communal idea in France in 1871." The International "possessed a ready-made organization, where the word 'commune' stood for the word 'section' and the federation of communes was nothing but a federation of sections."[45]

Compare this quotation with those of the English syndicalists of the 1830s, cited in the preceding chapter, who wanted to replace the bourgeois-parliamentary state with a *federation of trade-unions*. Let us recall the analogous theses of the French syndicalists in the twentieth century. And let us not forget that in our time, working people everywhere come to the idea of the "soviet state" after experiencing the soviets as *their own* combat organizations, created in the process of a class struggle that has taken revolutionary forms.

In all the communalist theses, it is common to deny that the "state" can be an instrument for the revolutionary transformation of society in the direction of socialism. However, Marxism, as it developed from 1848 onwards, is characterized above all by the fact that—following the tradition of Babeuf and Blanqui—it recognized the state (naturally after its conquest by the proletariat) as the principal lever of such a transformation. That is why, as early as the 1860s, the anarchists and Proudhonists considered Marx and Engels to be "statists." How, then, did they [Marx and Engels] react to the experience of the Paris Commune, when the proletariat attempted for the first time to exercise its dictatorship and embark on a socialist transformation?

12. Marx and the Commune

The Proudhonists and the anarchists, who were not well acquainted with the laws of economic development, imagined the process of transferring the means of production to the working class in a very naive and simplistic way. They did not see that capitalism had created such a grandiose mechanism of concentrated production and exchange that the working class cannot master it without having at its disposal an equally grandiose *administrative machinery*, extending over the entire economic sphere embraced by capital. Only by ignoring the whole complexity and magnitude of the social and revolutionary transformation could they imagine the self-sufficient "commune"—itself based on self-sufficient "autonomous" productive units—as the lever of such a transformation.

Of course, Marx was better informed than anyone about the decisive role played by anarcho-Proudhonism in the communist movement. As early as 1866, in a letter to Engels (20 June 1866), he refers ironically to "Proudhonized Stirnerianism," which is inclined to see "everything broken down into small *'groups'* or *'communes,'* which in turn form an *'association,'* but not a state."[46]

But in 1871, Marx's task was to defend the cause of the Commune from its arch-enemies. He faced the task of justifying the first attempt of the proletariat to gain power, an attempt that, had it not been crushed by external forces, would have led the workers beyond their original objectives and broken the ideological bonds that limited and distorted the scope of their revolution.

It is understandable, therefore, why in his defence of the Commune Marx did not even raise the question of whether the realization of socialism is conceivable within the framework of autonomous city and rural communes. In light of the existing division of labour, economic centralization, and the degree of development of the forces of production already attained at that time, merely to pose the question would have meant a categorical rejection of the notion that the autonomous commune could "solve the social question." It is understandable why Marx avoided the question of whether a federalist link between the communes could ensure, to some extent, planned social production on the broad basis prepared by capitalism. It is understandable why Marx touches only in passing on one of the most important issues of the social revolution—the relationship between the city and the countryside—and merely asserts, without *any* supporting evidence, that "the communal constitution brought the rural producers under the intellectual lead of the central towns of their districts, and there secured to them, in the working men, the natural trustees of their interests,"[47] whereas, on the contrary, the whole question is whether a socialist economy—involving economic leadership of the village by the city—can be placed within the framework of a federation of autonomous communes.

Marx could "push aside" all these questions in the expectation that, in the process of the social revolution, they would find their own solution, leaving behind the anarcho-communalist illusions with which the workers began the revolution.

But Marx did not merely remain silent on the Paris Commune's contradictions. He attempted to resolve these contradictions by recognizing the Commune as "the political form at last discovered under which to work out the economical emancipation of labour,"[48] and in so doing came into conflict with his own principle, that the lever of the social revolution can only be the conquest of *state power*.

"The Communal Constitution," declared Marx, "would have restored to the social body all the forces hitherto absorbed by the State parasite feeding upon, and clogging the free movement of society."[49]

"The very existence of the Commune," he says later, "involved , as a matter of course, local municipal liberty, but no longer as a check upon the, *now-superseded*, State power" (our emphasis, Martov).[50]

Thus, the destruction of the "bureaucratic-military machine" of the state, about which Marx writes in a letter to Kugelmann, morphed imperceptibly into the abolition of all state power, of any apparatus of coercion in the service of the social administration. Breaking up the "the modern state edifice"[51] of the Continental type became the decomposition of the state as such.

Are we dealing here with a certain deliberate vagueness of wording that allowed Marx to avoid touching on the weak points of the Paris Commune at a moment when the Commune was being trampled by triumphant reaction? Or did the powerful impulse of the revolutionary proletariat of Paris, marching under the banner of the Commune, make acceptable to Marx certain ideas of Proudhonist origin? Whatever the case, Bakunin and his friends saw Marx's *The Civil War in France* as an acknowledgement of the correctness of the very path of social revolution which they advocated. In his memoirs, James Guillaume observes with satisfaction that, in its assessment of the Commune, the General Council of the International (under whose auspices *The Civil War* was published) adopted the viewpoint of the federalists.[52] Bakunin declared triumphantly: "The effect of the communalist uprising was so great that even the Marxists were compelled to bow and scrape before it—because it had overthrown all their ideas—and contrary to any logic and their actual sentiments, appropriated its aims and program."[53] There is more than a little polemical exaggeration in these words, of course, but they do contain a grain of truth.

In the summer of 1917, it was precisely these not very definite opinions of Marx's on the destruction of the state by a proletarian uprising and the creation of the Commune, that formed the basis for the new revelation Lenin presented to the world concerning the tasks of the social revolution. It is precisely on the basis of these opinions of Marx, that Lenin constructed his anarcho-syndicalist scheme for the destruction of the state happening *in the very moment of the proletariat's conquest of the dictatorship, replacing the state* with the political "form 'at last discovered'" which in 1871 was imagined as the Commune and was now [imagined as] "the soviets," which after "the Russian Revolutions of 1905 and 1917, in different circumstances and under different conditions, continue the work of the Commune and confirm Marx's brilliant historical analysis."[54]

As early as 1899, in his well-known *The Preconditions of Socialism*, Eduard Bernstein observed that in *The Civil War* Marx took a step toward Proudhon. "Whatever other differences there may be between

Marx and 'petit-bourgeois' Proudhon, on this point their way of thinking is as nearly as possible the same."[55] Bernstein's words threw Lenin
into a rage. "Monstrous! Ridiculous! Renegade!" Lenin shouted at Bernstein, and he took the opportunity to revile Plekhanov and Kautsky for
not correcting "*this* distortion of Marx by Bernstein"[56] in their polemics
against Bernstein's book.[57]

But following his attack on Kautsky and Plekhanov, Lenin could
have also come down on the "Spartacist" Franz Mehring, unquestion-
ably the best expert and commentator on Marx. In his *Karl Marx: The
History of His Life*, published not long before his death, Mehring writes
categorically, leaving no room for doubt.

> The way in which the Address dealt with these details [about the
> Commune—Martov] was brilliant, but *there was a certain contra-
> diction between them and the opinions previously held by Marx and
> Engels for a quarter of a century and set down in* The Communist
> Manifesto.[58] They held that one of the final results of the future pro-
> letarian revolution would certainly be the dissolution of that political
> institution known as the state, but this dissolution was to have been
> gradual. The main aim of such an institution was always to protect
> by force of arms the economic oppression of the working majority of
> the population by a minority in exclusive possession of the wealth of
> society. With the disappearance of this minority of wealthy persons,
> the necessity for an armed repressive institution such as the state
> would also disappear. At the same time, however, they pointed out
> that, in order to achieve this and other still more important aims of
> the future social revolution, the working class must first seize the
> organized political power of the state and use it to crush the resist-
> ance of the capitalists and reorganize society. *These opinions of* The
> Communist Manifesto *could not be reconciled with the praise lavished
> by the Address of the General Council on the Paris Commune for the
> vigorous fashion in which it had begun to exterminate the parasitic state.*
> (Our emphasis throughout, Martov)[59]

And Mehring adds, "It is not difficult to realize that the supporters of Bakunin interpreted the Address of the General Council in their own way."[60]

Mehring believes that it was "perfectly clear" to Marx and Engels that there was a contradiction between the theses presented in *The Civil War* and their previous position on the conquest of state power. He writes, "After the death of Marx, Engels was compelled to engage in a struggle against the anarchist tendencies in the working-class movement, and he let this proviso drop and once again took his stand on the basis of *The Manifesto*."[61]

"On the basis of *The Manifesto*," the working class would seize the state apparatus that the bourgeoisie had created, *democratize* it from top to bottom (see the immediate measures that, according to *The Manifesto*, the proletariat would implement upon winning power), and *thereby* transform it from a machine used by the minority for the suppression of the majority into a machine for the suppression of a minority by the majority, for the emancipation of this majority from social inequality. That means, as Marx wrote in 1852, not merely to adopt and use the ready-made state machine of the bureaucratic, police, and military type, but to *smash* it in order to construct a new state machine based on the self-government of the people under the leadership of the proletariat.

The ambiguous formulations found in *The Civil War in France* were reasonable enough given the practical necessity for the General Council of the International to defend the cause of the Commune (a Commune led by Hébertists and Proudhonists) against its enemies. But these formulations almost completely erased the line between the Marxist thesis of the "conquest of political power" and the anarchist idea of the "destruction of the state." On the eve of the overturn of October 1917, in his struggle against the republican democratism practised by the socialist parties that he opposed, Lenin used these formulations to good effect, accumulating in his *The State and Revolution* as many contradictions as were found in the heads of all the members of the Commune put together: Jacobins, Blanquists, Hébertists, Proudhonists, and anarchists. Objectively (and most likely without Lenin's even realizing it), this was necessary so that an attempt to create a state machine very similar in its structure to the former military and bureaucratic type and in the hands of a small party,[62] might be presented to the masses—then in a seething, revolutionary state—as the destruction of the old state machinery, the birth of a *stateless* society based on a minimum of coercion and discipline.

At a time when the most revolutionary masses were expressing their emancipation from the centuries-old yoke of the old state by forming autonomous "Kronstadt republics" and carrying out experiments in "workers' control," which were understood in a completely anarchist sense, etc.—at that moment, the "dictatorship of the proletariat and the poor peasantry" (in the form of the actual dictatorship of the "true" spokespeople for the needs of these classes: the chosen ones of Bolshevik communism) could only be consolidated by dressing itself in this anarchist anti-state ideology. The formula of "All power to the soviets!" was the most suitable to give mystical expression to the contradictory desires of the revolutionary elements of the people: to create a machine that would suppress the exploiting classes to the benefit of the exploited; and, simultaneously to be free from *any* state machine, which *for them* would mean the necessity of subordinating their wills as individuals or groups to the will of the social whole.

The "soviet mysticism" current at this stage of the revolution in the countries of western Europe, is no different in origin and significance, while in Russia itself, the evolution of the soviet state has already led to the creation of a new and very complex state machine based on the very same antagonisms that characterize the state of the capitalist class—the opposition of the "administration of persons" to the "administration of things," the opposition of "administration" to "self-government," the opposition of the bureaucratic functionary to the citizen.

The economic retrogression that occurred during the world war *simplified* economic life in all countries and, in the consciousness of the masses, the question of the organization of production was eclipsed by the question of uniformity in distribution and consumption. This retrogression has revived in the working class the illusion that the national economy can be controlled by transferring the means of production directly—bypassing the state—to individual groups of workers ("workers' control," "immediate socialization," etc.).

From the soil of these resurgent economic illusions,[63] we see again the growth of the illusion that the emancipation of the working class can be realized, not by *conquering* the state, but by *destroying* it. Through these and other illusions, the revolutionary working class is thrown back toward the confusion, obscurity, and ideological immaturity that characterized it during the Commune of 1871.

In part by exploiting, in part by themselves falling victim to these illusions and this ideological immaturity, certain extremist minorities of the socialist proletariat seek to circumvent the difficulty of realizing a genuine class dictatorship under conditions where this class, having lost its internal unity in the crisis of the war, is incapable of directly fighting for revolutionary goals. In the end, this anarchist illusion in the destruction of the state covers for the desire to concentrate all the coercive power of the state in the hands of a proletarian minority, one that trusts neither in the objective logic of the revolution nor in the class consciousness of the proletarian majority, let alone the people's majority. Therefore, *compelled* by external conditions and the inner conditions of the proletariat, the idea of a fundamental rupture in principle with all the old bourgeois forms of revolution—[a rupture] in the form of a "system of soviets"—serves as a cover for methods of the struggle for power characteristic of the bourgeois revolutions. Those revolutions were always accomplished through the transfer of power—from one "conscious minority, relying on an unconscious majority"—to another.

Appendix

Marx and the Problem of the Dictatorship
of the Proletariat

I

In her polemic against Eduard Bernstein, Rosa Luxemburg was quite right when she wrote, "The necessity of the proletariat's seizing power was always unquestionable for Marx and Engels."[1] But the *conditions* under which this seizure of power was to be realized certainly did not appear quite the same to Marx and Engels at different periods of their lives.

"At the beginning of their activity," writes Kautsky in his recent article *Democracy and Dictatorship*, "Marx and Engels were at first strongly influenced by Blanquism, although from the very beginning they treated it critically. The dictatorship of the proletariat to which they aspired, still showed many Blanquist features in their early works."[2] This statement is not entirely accurate. Even if Marx—putting aside the petit-bourgeois revolutionism that in no small measure coloured both the ideology and politics of Blanquism—considered the Blanquists of 1848 to be a party representing the revolutionary French proletariat, there is insufficient evidence to show that Marx and Engels were under the ideological influence of Blanqui and his supporters. Kautsky correctly points out that Marx and Engels always had a quite critical attitude toward the Blanquists. Their initial views on the dictatorship of the proletariat were undoubtedly influenced by the *Jacobin* tradition of

1793, a tradition with which the Blanquists were imbued. The powerful historical example of the political dictatorship exercised during the Terror by the Parisian lower classes served Marx and Engels as a point of departure for their conception of the future conquest of political power by the proletariat.

In 1895 (in his preface to *Class Struggles in France*), Engels summed up the experience that he and his friend had gathered in the revolutions of 1848 and 1871: "The time of surprise attacks, of revolutions carried through by small conscious minorities *at the head of masses lacking consciousness is past*."[3] Engels acknowledged that, in the first period of their activity, he and Marx had in fact been concerned with the conquest of political power "by a small conscious minority at the head of masses lacking consciousness," in other words the repetition, in the nineteenth century, of the experience of the Jacobin dictatorship, with the role of the Jacobins and the Cordeliers taken by the conscious revolutionary elements of the proletariat, relying on the vague social ferment of the broad masses. With skilful policies and imbued with the understanding conferred by the practise and theory of scientific socialism, the vanguard in power should, on the day after the revolution, introduce the broad proletarian masses to the historical tasks of the revolution, and educate them to be conscious subjects of historical action. Only with such a conception of the dictatorship of the proletariat could Marx and Engels expect that the revolution of 1848—which began as the final struggle between feudal and bourgeois society, and with internal conflicts between individual strata of bourgeois society—would end after a more or less prolonged interval with the historic victory of the proletariat over bourgeois society.

In 1895, Engels recognized the inconsistency of this view. "Where it is a question of a complete transformation of the social organisation, the masses themselves must also be in on it, must themselves already have grasped what is at stake, what they are coming out for. The history of the last fifty years has taught us that."[4]

This is not to say, however, that in 1848 Marx and Engels in any way ignored the basic historical preconditions for socialist revolution. Not only did they recognize the need for capitalism to develop sufficiently to make possible a socialist transformation, but they also explicitly rejected the possibility of the proletariat retaining power in the absence of this precondition. In 1846, in his letter to Moses Hess, Wilhelm Weitling described his break with Marx in the following words: "We have come to the conclusion that there could be no question now of realizing communism in Germany; that first the bourgeoisie must seize power."⁵ The "we" here refers specifically to Marx and Engels, for Weitling goes on to say that "on this point Marx and Engels argued very sharply with me."⁶ In October and November of 1847, in his article "Moralizing Criticism," directed against Herzen, Marx wrote on this question with complete certainty:

> If the bourgeoisie is politically, that is, by its state power, "maintaining injustice in property relations" [Herzen's expression— Martov], it is not creating it. The "injustice in property relations" . . . by no means arises from the political rule of the bourgeois class, but vice versa, the political rule of the bourgeois class arises from these modern relations of production. . . . If therefore the proletariat overthrows the political rule of the bourgeoisie, *its victory will only be temporary, only an element in the service of the bourgeois revolution itself,* as in the year 1794, as long as in the course of history, in its "movement," the material conditions have not yet been created which make *necessary* the abolition of the bourgeois mode of production, and therefore also the definitive overthrow of the political rule of the bourgeoisie.⁷

Marx, then, allowed for the possibility of a political victory of the proletariat over the bourgeoisie at a point in historical development when the prerequisites for a socialist revolution were not yet mature. But such a victory, he said, would prove to be fleeting, and he predicted with ingenious foresight that such a premature—from a historical viewpoint—conquest of political power by the proletariat would "*only be . . . an element in the service of* the bourgeois revolution." We must conclude, therefore, that, in the case of an obviously premature conquest of power, Marx would consider it obligatory for the conscious elements of the proletariat to pursue a policy that takes account of the fact that such a conquest objectively represents "only *an element in the service of* the bourgeois revolution" and would serve the latter by aiding its further development, a policy based on the "self-limitation" of the proletariat in defining and resolving revolutionary tasks. For the proletariat will be able to score a real victory over the bourgeoisie—instead of for the bourgeoisie—only when "in the course of history, in its 'movement', the material conditions have ... been created which make *necessary* [not merely objectively *possible!*—Martov] the elimination of the bourgeois mode of production."

The following words from Marx make it clear the sense in which a temporary victory of the proletariat could prove to be a moment in the development of the bourgeois revolution:

> The terror in France could thus by its mighty hammer-blows only serve to spirit away, as it were, the ruins of feudalism from French soil. The timidly considerate bourgeoisie would not have accomplished this task in decades. The bloody action of the people thus only prepared the way for it.[8]

The Reign of Terror in France was the temporary domination of the petit-bourgeois democracy and the proletariat over all the propertied classes, including the genuine bourgeoisie. Marx indicates very clearly that such temporary domination cannot serve as a starting point for a socialist transformation until the material conditions making this transformation necessary have developed. Marx seems to be writing specifically for the benefit of those people who consider the fact that the petit-bourgeois democracy and the proletariat can seize power, as proof that society is ripe for a socialist revolution. At the same time, however, he writes as if for the benefit of those socialists who see a radical contradiction between the fact of a revolution that is bourgeois in its objectives, and the fact that in the course of its very development power might escape (temporarily) from the hands of the bourgeoisie and pass into the hands of the democratic masses—or for the benefit of those socialists who consider utopian the mere idea of such a displacement of power and who do not realize that this phenomenon is "only an element in the service of the bourgeois revolution," ensuring, under certain circumstances, a more complete and more radical removal of the obstacles in its [the bourgeois revolution's] path.

II

The European revolution of 1848 did not lead to the conquest of political power by the proletariat. Soon after the June Days, Marx and Engels began to realize that the historical conditions for such a conquest were not yet ripe. However, as is well known, overestimating the pace of historical development, they expected a new revolutionary upsurge in the coming years, even before the last wave of the 1848 crisis had subsided. They saw new factors that seemed to favour the possibility of political power passing into the hands of the proletariat, not only in the rich experience it had acquired in the class struggles during the "mad year"[9] but also in the evolution experienced by the petite bourgeoisie, which—in their opinion—was being pushed irresistibly toward a lasting alliance with the proletariat.

In his *Class Struggles in France* and later in the *Eighteenth Brumaire*, Marx noted the movement toward the proletariat of the urban democratic petite bourgeoisie, a movement that took definite form by 1848. And in the second of the books mentioned, he announced the probability of a similar movement on the part of the small-holding peasants, as a result of their disillusionment with the dictatorship of Napoleon III, whose principal creators and strongest support they had been. Marx wrote:

> The interests of the peasants, therefore, are no longer, as under Napoleon, in accord with, but in opposition to the interests of the bourgeoisie, to capital. Hence the peasants find their natural ally and leader in the *urban proletariat*, whose task is the overthrow of the bourgeois order.[10]

The proletariat, therefore, did not have to "wait" until it became a decisive majority in order to win political power. In addition to the growth resulting from the development of capitalism, it benefitted from the disintegration of the foundations of private property, alienating the small property-holders of the city and the countryside from the capitalist bourgeoisie. When the revolutionary process—halted due to self-exhaustion—resumed twenty years later, leading to the creation of the Paris Commune, Marx saw in this new fact an opportunity favouring the completion of this uprising in the real and lasting dictatorship of the proletariat. Marx wrote in *The Civil War in France*:

> This was the first revolution in which the working class was openly acknowledged as the only class capable of social initiative, even by the great bulk of the Parisian Third Estate—shopkeepers, tradesmen, merchants—the wealthy capitalists alone excepted.... In 1848, the same portion of the Third Estate had assisted in putting down the working men's insurrection of June 1848, then immediately was unceremoniously sacrificed to their creditors by the Constituent Assembly.... This mass of the Third Estate felt it had to choose either the Commune or the Empire.... After the exodus from Paris of the high Bonapartist and capitalist *Bohême*, the true middle-class Party of Order came out under the name of the "Union républicaine," enrolling themselves under the colours of the Commune and defending it against the wilful slander of Thiers.[11]

As early as 1844, when he was still only making his way toward socialism, Marx defined, in his *Introduction to the Critique of Hegel's Philosophy of Law*, the conditions under which the revolutionary class could lay claim to a leading position in society. For that, "*one* estate" must be recognized by all the masses oppressed under the existing regime as "*par excellence* the estate of liberation." This situation is possible when the estate against which the struggle is led becomes, in the eyes of the masses, "the obvious estate of oppression."[12] In 1848, this situation certainly did not exist. The decomposition of small property was not yet far enough advanced.

The situation appeared substantially different in 1871. By that time, Marx and Engels had undoubtedly freed themselves from all influence of the Jacobin tradition and, therefore, from the conception of the dictatorship of a "conscious minority" acting at the head of the unconscious [i.e., simply outraged—Martov] masses. It is precisely on the phenomenon of the ruined small property-holders consciously rallying around the socialist proletariat that the two great theoreticians of scientific socialism based their forecast of the success of the Parisian insurrection, which, as we know, began against their wishes. They were undoubtedly correct concerning the *urban* petite bourgeoisie (at least, that of Paris). Unlike the June Days, the massacre of the Communards was not the work of the entire bourgeois society but only of its capitalist classes. The petite bourgeoisie had no part in the suppression of the Commune nor in the orgy of reaction that followed. They were, however, much less correct when assessing the situation with regard to the peasantry. In *The Civil War*, Marx presumed that only the isolation of Paris from the provinces and the brevity of the Commune's existence had prevented the peasants from joining with the proletarian revolution. Pursuing a line of reasoning begun in the *Eighteenth Brumaire*, he said:

> The peasant was a Bonapartist, because the great Revolution, with all its benefits to him, was in his eyes personified in Napoleon. This self-delusion had almost entirely disappeared under the Second Empire. This prejudice of the past could not withstand the appeal of the Commune, which appealed to the living interests and the urgent needs of the peasantry. The Rurals (as the agrarians, who sat on the National Assembly, were called at that time) knew too well that if Communal Paris communicated freely with the provinces, a general rising of the peasants would break out in just three months.[13]

The history of the Third Republic has shown that Marx was wrong on this point. In the 1870s, the peasantry (as well as a significant section of the urban petite bourgeoisie in the provinces) was still far from such a break with capital and the bourgeoisie. They were still far from recognizing the latter as the "oppressing class," far from considering the proletariat as "the liberating class" and handing over to it the leadership of their movement. In 1895, in his introduction to *Class Struggles*, Engels had to state: "Once again it was proved how impossible even then, twenty years after the time described in our work [1848–51], this rule of the working class was," because "France left Paris in the lurch." (On the other hand, as a cause of the defeat, Engels pointed to the lack of internal unity in the very ranks of the insurgent proletariat, to its still insufficient revolutionary maturity, thanks to which it wasted its strength in "fruitless strife between the two parties which split it, the Blanquists (the majority) and the Proudhonists (the minority)."[14])

But no matter how mistaken Marx was in his assessment of the real balance of forces, in 1871 he outlined very clearly the problem of the dictatorship of the proletariat. "The Commune," he wrote, was "the true representative of all the healthy elements of French society, and therefore the truly *national government*."[15] Therefore, according to Marx, the dictatorship of the proletariat does not consist in the proletariat suppressing all non-proletarian classes in society. On the contrary, it means the proletariat rallying around itself all the "healthy elements" of society—all except the "rich capitalists," all except the class against which the historic struggle of the proletariat is directed. Both in its composition and in its tendencies, the government of the Commune was a workers' government. But this government was an expression of the dictatorship of the proletariat not because it was *imposed* by violence on the majority of non-proletarian masses. It was a proletarian dictatorship because those workers and those "acknowledged representatives of the working class" had derived *their power from that majority*. "The Commune," Marx stressed, "was formed of the municipal councillors, chosen by universal suffrage in the various wards of the town. . . ."

> While the merely oppressive organs of the old governmental power were to be amputated, its legitimate functions were to be wrested from an authority usurping pre-eminence over society itself, and restored to the responsible agents of society. . . . universal suffrage was to serve the people, constituted in Communes [outside of Paris]

as individual suffrage serves every other employer in the search for
the workmen and managers in his business."[16]

The consistently democratic organization of the Commune, based
on universal suffrage, the immediate recall of every elected representative by decision of the electorate, the absence of a bureaucratic caste
and an armed force separated from the people, the fact that all offices
were subject to election—that is what constitutes, according to Marx,
the essence of the class dictatorship of the proletariat. He does not
speak of any *opposition* between [such a] dictatorship and democracy.
In 1847, in his original draft of *The Communist Manifesto*, Engels wrote:

> In the first place, it [the proletarian revolution] will inaugurate a
> *democratic constitution* and thereby, directly or indirectly, the political
> rule of the proletariat. Directly in England, where the proletariat
> already constitutes the majority of the people. Indirectly in France
> and in Germany, where the majority of the people consists not only
> of proletarians but also of small peasants and urban petit-bourgeois,
> who are only now being proletarianized and in all their political
> interests are becoming more and more dependent on the proletar-
> iat and therefore soon will have to conform to the demands of the
> proletariat.[17]

The first step in the workers' revolution, declares the *Manifesto*, "is to
raise the proletariat to the position of ruling class, to win the battle of
democracy."[18]

Marx and Engels equate the transformation of the proletariat into
the ruling class with the achievement of democracy. It is only in the
form of a consistent democracy that they envisaged the proletariat exercising its political authority.

As Marx and Engels became convinced that socialism could win only
by relying on the *majority* of the people *consciously* sympathizing with
the positive program of socialism, any Jacobin content was erased from
their ideas of a class dictatorship. But what positive content remains in
the concept of dictatorship once it has been modified in this manner?
Exactly that which was formulated quite precisely in the program of

our party [the Russian Social Democratic Labour Party, RSDRP], a program drafted at a time when the theoretical disputes provoked by "Bernsteinism" prompted Marxists to polish and define with precision certain terms that had lost a considerable amount of concrete meaning through long, uncritical use in everyday political struggles.

The program of the RSDRP was the only official program of a workers' party to formulate the idea of the conquest of political power by the proletariat in the terms of a "class dictatorship." It was the persistent desire of Bernstein, Jaurès, and other critics of Marxism to attach the term "dictatorship of the proletariat" to the Blanquist meaning of power, that which is held by the violence of an organized minority and resting on violence exercised by this minority over the majority. For this reason, the authors of the Russian program had to delineate as precisely as possible the limits of this political concept. They did this by saying that the dictatorship of the proletariat is that power which is capable of crushing all resistance of the exploiting classes to revolutionary socialist transformation.

And that is all. An effective force concentrated in the state power [*vlast*], capable of carrying out the *conscious will of the majority* against the resistance of an economically powerful minority—in this way, and only in this way, does the meaning of "dictatorship of the proletariat" align with the teachings of Marx. Not only can such a dictatorship be reconciled with democratic rule, it can only exist within the framework of democracy—that is, only if complete political equality for all citizens is assured. Such a dictatorship is conceivable only insofar as the proletariat has rallied around itself "all the healthy elements of the nation"—that is, all those who cannot but benefit from the revolutionary transformation outlined in the program of the proletariat, when historical development has led all the healthy elements to a consciousness of their interests. A government embodying such a dictatorship would be, in the full sense of the word, a "national government."

Notes

Introduction

1. Michel Surya, Georges *Bataille: An Intellectual Biography*, 160.

   Boris Souvarine (né Boris Konstantinovich Lifschits, 1895-1984) was a cofounder of the French Communist Party and, from May 1921 until January 1925, a resident in Moscow—where he "became a member of three of the leading bodies of the Comintern," acronym for the Third or Communist International. Ibid., 161.

   In the early years following the Russian Revolution of 1917, the name of Leon Trotsky (né Lev Davidovich Bronstein, 1879-1940) was as widely known as that of Vladimir Lenin (né Vladimir Il'ich Ul'ianov, 1870-1924). From the mid-1920s on, Trotsky came to symbolize the socialist opposition to Stalin and Stalinism. A victim of Stalin's Great Terror, Trotsky was forcibly exiled from the Soviet Union in 1929 and assassinated by a Soviet agent in 1940. Unlike many victims of the Great Terror, he has never been "rehabilitated." Nelson P. Lande, "Posthumous Rehabilitation and the Dust-Bin of History," 267.

   Alexander (or Solomon) Lozovskii (né Solomon Abramovich Dridzo, 1878-1952), is best known for his leading role in the Red International of Labour Unions (RILU). During the world war—in exile in Paris, along with Martov, Trotsky and others—he collaborated in the anti-war publication launched under the name *Golos* (The Voice). Arrested in 1949 on fabricated (and antisemitic) charges, he was executed in

1952—posthumously rehabilitated. Albert Resis, "Lozovskii, A," in *The Modern Encyclopedia of Russian and Soviet History* (hereafter *MERSH*), 20: 167–70); Reiner Tosstorff, *The Red International of Labour Unions (RILU) 1920-1937*, 821–32.

2. Israel Getzler, *Martov: A Political Biography of a Russian Social Democrat*, 232–33.

3. Iulii Martov, *Izbrannoe* [Selected works], 645.

4. *The Mensheviks in the Russian Revolution*, edited by Abraham Ascher (with translations by Paul Stevenson), provides a small selection of Martov's writings; see also *Martov and Zinoviev: Head to Head in Halle*, edited by Ben Lewis. For the Martov material on the Marxists Internet Archive, see https://www.marxists.org/archive/martov/index.htm.

5. V. Ia. Zevin and T. V. Panchenko, "Lenin, Works of," from *The Great Soviet Encyclopedia*, https://encyclopedia2.thefreedictionary.com/Lenin%2c+Works+of.

6. "Index Translationum: 'Top 50' Author," UNESCO, accessed 29 October 2018, http://www.unesco.org/xtrans/bsstatexp.aspx?crit1L=5&nTyp=min&topN=50. The database compiles information received from 1980 to the present, although most of the published information dates to no later than 2010.

7. Alexander Potressov [Potresov], "Lenin: Versuch einer Charakterisierung" [Lenin: An attempt at a Characterization], 415.

    Alexander Nikolaevich Potresov (pseudonym Starover, 1869-1934) in 1895 "helped establish the St. Petersburg League of Struggle for the Emancipation of the Working Class with Martov and Vladimir Lenin." Potresov divided from Lenin in 1903 and drifted apart from Martov after 1905. He supported Russia during the world war. Jonathan Davis, *Historical Dictionary of the Russian Revolution* (hereafter *HDRR*), 189 and 208–9.

8. Raphael R. Abramovitch, *The Soviet Revolution, 1917–1939*, 18–21.

    Raphael R. Abramovitch (Rafail Abramovich, né Rein, also known as Rein-Abramovich, 1880-1963), was a leading member of both the Mensheviks and the Bund—from the Yiddish word for "union", shorthand for the General Jewish Labour Bund in Lithuania, Poland, and Russia, first mass working class party in the Russian empire. *HDRR*, 23 and 72.

9. During the late eighteenth-century revolution in France, the Jacobin clubs according to Paul Hanson "were the most important of the popular societies ... By early 1790 there were roughly 1,000 members in the Paris club, and that number more than doubled by June 1791." The Jacobins achieved the peak of their influence during the "Jacobin dictatorship" beginning in April 1793 when the Committee of Public Safety became the executive power in the French government. The dictatorship presided over the peak of the Great Terror in 1793 and 1794. Albert Soboul says that during the Terror, between 100,000 and 300,000 people were detained and between 35,000 and 40,000 executed. Paul R. Hanson, *Historical Dictionary of the French Revolution* (hereafter *HDFR*), 74-76, 167; Albert Soboul, *Précis d'histoire de la révolution française*, 321–22.

10. Getzler, Martov, 37.

11. V. Markus and R. Senkus, "Kharkiv."

12. Getzler, Martov, 192.

13. Dmitrii Dobrovol'skii and Liudmila Peppel', "Revoliutsiia, vosstanie, perevorot: Semantika i pragmatika" [Revolution, uprising, overturn: Semantics and pragmatics], 91.

14. Ibid., 90.

15. Ibid., 78–79.

16. The distinctions between *revoliutsiia* [revolution], *perevorot* [overturn] and *vosstanie* [uprising] are quite different today than they were in Martov's time. "Many of the distinctions" between these three words "typical of modern usage, turn out to be uncharacteristic for the use of these words at the beginning of the 20th century ... there have been significant shifts in their meaning over the last hundred years." Dobrovol'skii and Peppel', 99.

17. Leopold H. Haimson, *The Making of Three Russian Revolutionaries: Voices from the Menshevik Past*, 19.

18. By "Extraordinary Commissions," Martov is referring to the first iteration of the post-revolutionary secret police, the All-Russian Extraordinary Commission for Combating Counter-Revolution and Sabotage, the institution that we now know as the Cheka. *HDRR*, 75–76.

19. Iulii Martov, "Doloi smertnuiu kazn'!" [Down with the death penalty!] (July 1918), in Martov, *Izbrannoe* [Selected works], 375, 379.

20. N. N. Sukhanov, *Zapiski o revoliutsii* [Notes on the revolution], 7:226. Compare with Sukhanov, *The Russian Revolution, 1917: A Personal Record*, 649–50.

    Nikolai Nikolaevich Sukhanov (né Gimmer, 1882-?) was a founding member of the Petrograd Soviet in 1917. His *Zapiski o revoliutsii* (Notes on the Revolution)—seven-volumes and approximately 2,700 pages in the original Russian—"has placed scholars in his debt and has made Sukhanov known to history." The Notes—in which he described Joseph Stalin as a "grey blur"— undoubtedly played a role in his arrest in the late 1920s and prosecution in the Menshevik trial in 1931, one of a series of show trials carried out in the Soviet Union (trials which have now all been completely discredited). Sent to the Gulag along with thousands of other political prisoners, the circumstances of his death are unknown. John D. Basil, "Sukhanov, Nikolai Nikolaevich," in *MERSH*, 38: 25–28.

    The two papers referred to were both liberal in the sense that they expressed views supporting the positions of the Kadets (acronym for Konstitutsionno-demokraticheskaia partiia or Constitutional-Democratic Party). They were both mass-circulation daily papers, a survey published in May 1916 indicating that *Sovremennoe slovo* had a daily circulation of 76,000, *Rech* 45,000. "News from Russia," 248.

    The term *auto-da-fé*—used here by Sukhanov in a bitterly sarcastic manner—refers to a practice which Francisco Bethencourt says dates from "the medieval Inquisition" that "used its elaborate ceremonies to emphasize the triumph of Catholic faith over heresy." Francisco Bethencourt, "The *Auto da Fé*: Ritual and Imagery," 155.

21. Central Committee of the Russian Social Democratic Workers' Party (United), "Suppression of the Press," 107–8. The committee to which this translation refers is usually translated as the "Military Revolutionary Committee."

22. The Social (or Socialist) Revolutionary (SR) Party (formally the *Partiia sotsialistov-revoliutsionerov* or PSR) was "the most important non-Bolshevik socialist party in Russia from about 1901 to 1921." It had "possibly a million members at its peak." Its internationalist (anti-war) minority separated from the majority between February and October 1917. The new party, the Left SRs, governed together with the Bolsheviks in a short-lived coalition government from the end of 1917 to March 1918. Maureen Perrie, "Socialist Revolutionary Party," in *MERSH*, 36: 95–102.

23. Getzler, *Martov*, 181, 182.
24. Abramovitch, *The Soviet Revolution, 1917–1939*, 165.
25. F. Dan, *Dva goda skitani (1918-1921)* [Two years of wandering (1918-1921)]. Berlin: 1922, 13, 14. Quoted in David Dallin, "Between the World War and the NEP," 227.

    Fedor Il'ich Dan (né Gurvich, 1871-1947) was a physician by profession, and a leading member of the Russian Marxist left from the mid-1890s until his death. He worked closely with Martov, taking an internationalist (anti-war) position during the world war. John D. Basil, "Dan, Fedor Il'ich," in *MERSH*, 8: 162–65.

    Viktor Mikhailovich Chernov (1873-1952) was a founder of the SRs, its leading ideologist and theoretician. During the world war, Chernov was part of the internationalist (anti-war) minority inside the party. He was elected in 1917 to the Petrograd Soviet's Central Executive Committee, becoming its deputy chairman, and was elected president for the one and only session of the Constituent Assembly, forcibly disbanded by the Bolsheviks in January 1918. Maureen Perrie, "Chernov, Viktor Mikhailovich," in *MERSH*, 7: 4–7.
26. Dallin, "Between the World War and the NEP," 228.

    In fact, we now know that later that decade, there were mass oppositional meetings organized by the anti-Stalinist United Opposition. Ivan Khoroshev (writing under the pseudonym Mikhail Nil'skii) reports that in the Autumn of 1927, opposition students took over "the largest auditorium of the Moscow Higher Technical School" as the venue for a 3,000 strong meeting which heard speeches from United Opposition leaders Leon Trotsky, Lev Kamenev and Grigory Zinoviev. Mikhail Nil'skii [Ivan Mitrofanovich Khoroshev], *Vorkuta*, 74–78.

    Lev Borisovich Kamenev (né Rozenfel'd, 1883–1936) and Grigory Evseevich Zinoviev (né Radomysl'skii, 1883–1936) were "Old Bolsheviks" and among Lenin's closest associates. Both became victims of the Great Terror under Stalin and were executed in August 1936—belatedly "rehabilitated" in 1988. R.C. Elwood, "Kamenev, Lev Borisovich," in *MERSH*, 15: 212–17; *HDRR*, 313–17. Lande, "Posthumous Rehabilitation and the Dust-Bin of History," 267.
27. Iosif Vissarionovich Stalin (né I. V. Dzhugashivili, 1879–1953) was born in Georgia and became a leading member of the Bolsheviks. He "did not distinguish himself in the October Revolution" but emerged in the

1920s as the dominant figure in the Soviet government, a position he was to hold until his death in 1953. Revered by many, including through a cult of personality which is "usually dated from his fiftieth birthday in 1929" Stalin has also been associated with the horrors of the 1930s – the "liquidation of the kulaks as a class," the rise of the gulag forced labour system of mass incarceration, and the years of the terror. Robert McNeal, "Stalin, Iosif Vissarionovich," in *MERSH*, 37: 63–72.

28. Raphael Abramowitsch [Abramovitch], Vassily Suchomlin, and Iraklii Zeretelli [Tsereteli], *Der Terror Gegen Die Sozialistischen Parteien in Russland Und Georgien* [The Terror against Socialist Parties in Russia and Georgia]. Portions of this, at the time, were translated into English. [Raphael R. Abramovitch], *Bolshevik Terror Against Socialists*.

29. Applebaum, *Gulag: A History*, 20.

30. An approach to politics first developed by Kimberle Crenshaw, "Demarginalizing the Intersection of Race and Sex"; Crenshaw, "Mapping the Margins."

31. Getzler, *Martov*, 19–20.

32. Ibid., 21.

33. Ibid., 1.

34. Ibid., 22.

35. Ibid., 24.

36. Ibid.

37. Sidney Hook, "Introduction," in Abramovitch, *The Soviet Revolution, 1917–1939*, viii.

38. Potressov, "Lenin," 412.

39. V. I. Lenin, "S chego nachat'?" [Where to begin?], *Iskra*, no. 4 (May 1901), in *Polnoe sobranie sochinenii* [The complete collected works] (hereafter *PSS*), 5:11–12. For the standard English translation, see *Lenin: Collected Works* (hereafter *LCW*), 5:22–23.

40. P. Iu. Savel'ev and S. V. Tiutiukin, "Iulii Osipovich Martov (1873–1923): The Man and the Politician," 18.

41. Getzler, *Martov*, 81.

42. Rossiiskaia sotsial-demokraticheskaia rabochaia partiia [Russian Social Democratic Labour Party], 1903, *Second Ordinary Congress of the RSDLP*, 529n7.

The translator, Brian Pearce, has chosen to take the acronym for the party from its English translation, rather than the Russian transliteration, hence RSDLP as opposed to RSDRP.

43. Nadezhda K. Krupskaya, *Memories of Lenin*, 75. In this translation, the name Bauman is written "Baumann."

Nadezhda Konstantinovna Krupskaya (1869-1939) was a senior Bolshevik leader, as well as being life partner with Lenin. Co-founder in 1910 of what is today known as International Women's Day, in 1914, she helped to establish the newspaper *Rabotnitsa* (The Woman Worker). Krupskaya was briefly a member of the anti-Stalinist opposition. *HDRR*, 165–66.

In 1926, according to Trotsky, "Krupskaya said, in a circle of Left Oppositionists: 'If Ilyich [Lenin] were alive, he would probably already be in prison'" Leon Trotsky, *The Revolution Betrayed*, 93–94.

Pavel Borisovich Axelrod (1850-1928) grew up in a poor Jewish family in the Ukrainian town of Pochep. In 1883, together with Georgii Plekhanov and Vera Zasulich, he helped found the first Russian Marxist organization, the Group for the Emancipation of Labour. In 1900 Axelrod helped Martov, Lenin and Potresov found *Iskra*. After the 1903 division, Ascher says that: "For the next two and a half decades Axelrod was the oustanding ideologist though not necessarily the most influential political leader, of Menshevism." Sukhanov calls him the "founder of Russian Social-Democracy." Abraham Ascher, "Axelrod, Pavel Borisovich," in *MERSH*, 2: 197–203; Sukhanov, *The Russian Revolution, 1917: A Personal Record*, 351. Leopold H. Haimson, *The Russian Marxists and the Origins of Bolshevism*, 26.

44. Getzler, *Martov*, 66.

45. Tony Cliff, *Lenin*, vol. 1, *Building the Party*, 98–139.

46. Lars T. Lih, *Lenin Rediscovered: What Is to Be Done? in Context*, 495.

47. Haimson, *The Making of Three Russian Revolutionaries: Voices from the Menshevik Past*, 482 n13.

48. Pavel Axelrod, "Ob'edinenie rossiiskoi sotsial-demokratii i ee zadachi" [The Unification of Russian social democracy and its tasks]. 15 December 1903 and 15 January 1904. An abridged version of this article exists in English translation but does not include the section here quoted. *The Mensheviks in the Russian Revolution*, edited by Abraham Ascher, 48–52.

49. Leon Trotsky, *Nashi politicheskie zadachi* [Our political tasks], 25; Compare with Trotsky, *Our Political Tasks*, 39.
50. Trotsky, *Nashi politicheskie zadachi* [Our political tasks], 68.
51. Potressov, "Lenin," 413.
52. V. I. Lenin, "A. M. Kalmykovoy" [To A. M. Kalmykova] (1903 first published 1927), in *PSS*, 46:301. Compare with "To Alexandra Kalmykova," in *LCW*, 34:168–70.
53. Potressov, "Lenin," 407.
54. Ibid., 413.
55. Ibid., 417.

Vera Ivanovna Zasulich (1849-1919), a populist in her youth, attained notoriety in 1878 for the attempted assassination of the Governor of St. Petersburg. On the editorial board of *Iskra* from 1900 to 1905, in 1912, she aligned with Plekhanov, and in 1914, supported Russia in the world war. *HDRR* 310-15; Michael Ellman, "Zasulich, Vera Ivanovna."

56. Lenin, "A. M. Kalmykovoy" [To A. M. Kalmykova] in *PSS*, 46:301. Getzler renders the first phrase "scourge and monster" (*Martov*, 67), while the standard translation offers "flayers and monsters" (*LCW*, 34:169). "Scourge" is somewhat better than "flayer," but both have an archaic feel to them.

Georgii Valentinovich Plekhanov (1856–1918), is often called the "Father of Russian Marxism." In 1883, together with Axelrod and Zasulich, he helped found the first Russian Marxist organization, the Emancipation of Labour Group (or Group for the Emancipation of Labour). In 1900, he assisted Lenin, Martov and Potresov in the launching of *Iskra*. In the world war, he supported Russia and its allies against Germany. Samuel H. Baron, "Plekhanov, Georgii Valentinovich," in *MERSH*, 28: 126–30.

57. Lydia [Lidiia] Osipovna Dan, 'Tenth Interview', 181–82.

Dan, Lidiia Osipovna (née Tsederbaum, 1878-1963), served on the editorial board of *Iskra* from 1901 until she was arrested in 1902 and banished to Siberia. After escaping in 1904, she resumed her role on *Iskra*. Internationalist during the war, she was expelled from Russia in 1922 for opposing Bolshevik policies. She was the sister of Martov, and life partner with Fedor Dan. "Dan, Lidiia Osipovna," in *MERSH*, 8: 165–66.

58. Getzler, *Martov*, 66–67; The interview with Dan uses "Mitrov" rather than "Metrov". Another account that reads very similarly, is in Jane Casey's fictionalized biography of Krupskaya, *I, Krupskaya: My Life with Lenin*, 179-86.

59. Dan, 'Tenth Interview', 181–82.

60. Getzler, *Martov*, 66.

61. Ibid.

62. V. I. Lenin and G. V. Plekhanov, "Proekt osobogo mneniia po delu N. E. Baumana" [Draft dissenting opinion in the N.E. Bauman case].

63. Quoted in ibid.

64. Lenin, "A. M. Kalmykovoy," 301. For the English translation used here, see Lenin, "To Alexandra Kalmykova," in *LCW*, 34:169. Getzler's translation reads "sheer obstinacy and threats of making it a public issue." Getzler, *Martov*, 67.

65. Abraham Ascher, *The Revolution of 1905: Russia in Disarray*, 1994, 1:262–63.

66. Orlando Figes, *A People's Tragedy: The Russian Revolution, 1891-1924*, 198–99.

67. Potressov, "Lenin," 417.

68. Barbara Ryan, "Personal Is Political," 2.

69. Abigail Bakan has, with tongue only partly in cheek, called our attention to the way in which this creates problems for the Left with her coining of the phrase "Communist Urgent Man," which she uses to describe someone who too often devolves into simply a small group bully. See Bakan, "Marxism, Feminism, and Epistemological Dissonance."

70. Bruno Naarden, *Socialist Europe and Revolutionary Russia: Perception and Prejudice*, 1848–1923, 274.

71. Getzler, *Martov*, 144–45.

72. Savel'ev and Tiutiukin, "Iulii Osipovich Martov," 40.

73. James D. White, *Lenin: The Practice and Theory of Revolution*, 108. Among those involved were—Antonov-Ovseenko, Kollontai, Larin, Lozovskii, Lunacharshky, Manuilskii, Martynov, Pavlovich, Pokrovskii, Trotsky, Uritskii, and Zalewski.

74. Savel'ev and Tiutiukin, "Iulii Osipovich *Martov*," 40.

75. Alfred Erich Senn, "The Politics of *Golos* and *Nashe Slovo*," 675-76; White, *Lenin*, 108.

76. Isaac Deutscher, *The Prophet Armed*, 216, quoting *Golos*, no. 38 (27 October 1914).

77. Victor Serge, *Memoirs of a Revolutionary*, 128.

   Victor Serge (né Victor Lvovich Khibalchich, 1890-1947), was born in Belgium to Russian emigré parents. Before the world war he was a libertarian anarchist. In exile in Russia in 1919, he became a prominent supporter of the Bolsheviks, with a particularly key role in the Communist International. David M. Walker and Daniel Gray, *Historical Dictionary of Marxism* (hereafter *HDM*), 283–84.

   A member of the anti-Stalinist opposition in the 1920s, he spent time in the Gulag, until being expelled from the Soviet Union just prior to the years of the Great Terror and mass execution of oppositionists. He famously broke with Trotsky in the 1930s over the 1921 Kronstadt uprising. Serge, "A Letter and Some Notes."

78. Getzler, Martov, 4, quoting Iulii Martov, *Zapiski sotsial-demokrata* [Memoirs of a social-democrat]. (Berlin-Petersburg-Moscow, 1922), 18.

79. Ibid., 4, quoting Martov, *Zapiski sotsial-demokrata* [Memoirs of a social-democrat],19.

80. Ibid., 4, 5.

81. Ibid., 4n23, quoting L. O. Dan, "Sem'ia (iz vospominanii)" [The Family: Fragments from memory], in Grigorii Aronson, ed., *Martov i ego blizkie: Sbornik* [Martov and his circle: a Compilation], New York: s.n., 11.

82. Ibid., 218–19.

83. Leon Trotsky, "Martov," in Trotsky, *Politicheskie siluety* [Political profiles], 66–67. Originally published in Trotsky, *Voina i revoliutsiia* [War and revolution]. Petrograd: Gosudarstvennoe izdatel'stvo [State publishing house], 1922.

84. Leon Trotsky, *The History of the Russian Revolution*, vol. 3, *Triumph of the Soviets*, 311.

85. Ben Lewis "The four-hour speech and the significance of Halle," 27.

86. Ben Lewis, ed., *Martov and Zinoviev: Head to Head in Halle*, 166.

87. China Miéville, *October: The Story of the Russian Revolution*, 12.

88. The qualifier "for a time" is necessary because "original copies of Trotsky's *Sochineniia* must be regarded as extremely rare." https://www.trotskyana.net/Leon_Trotsky/Sochineniia/sochineniia.html

89. Leon Trotsky, "Beglye mysli o G. V. Plekhanove" [Passing thoughts on G. V. Plekhanov], in Trotsky, *Politicheskie siluety* [Political profiles], 59.

90. I. M. Pavlov, "Primechaniia" [Notes], in Trotsky, *Politicheskie siluety* [Political profiles], 334 n46.

91. Leon Trotsky, "Negodiai" [The scoundrel] and "Ostav'te nas v pokoe" [Leave us alone], both in Trotsky, *Politicheskie siluety* [Political profiles], 68–69 and 62–64, respectively. "Negodiai" was first published in the 22 October 1916 issue of *Nachalo* [The beginning], while "Ostav'te nas v pokoe" appeared a year earlier, in the 14 October 1915 issue of *Nashe slovo* [Our word].

92. Trotsky, "Martov," 66–67.

93. Leon Trotsky, "Ot avtora" [From the author], in Trotsky, *Politicheskie siluety* [Political profiles], v.

94. See "Leon Trotsky: Political Profiles," Marxists Internet Archive, 2007, https://www.marxists.org/archive/trotsky/profiles/index.htm.

95. Lewis "The four-hour speech," 8.

96. Grigory Zinoviev, "Twelve Days in Germany," 67 and 91.

97. Lewis "The four-hour speech," 30.

98. Lih, "Martov in Halle," 161.

99. Naarden, *Socialist Europe and Revolutionary Russia*, 413.

100. Savel'ev and Tiutiukin, "Iulii Osipovich Martov (1873–1923)," 81; Jane Burbank, *Intelligentsia and Revolution: Russian Views of Bolshevism, 1917–1922*, 272.

101. Savel'ev and Tiutiukin, "Iulii Osipovich Martov (1873–1923)," 81.

102. Getzler, *Martov*, 212.

103. Ibid.

104. Savel'ev and Tiutiukin, "Iulii Osipovich Martov (1873–1923)," 83–84.

105. André Liebich, *From the Other Shore: Russian Social Democracy after 1921*, 1. According to Liebich: "Every document published in *Vestnik* in the 1920s relating to the intra-Bolshevik struggle has proven authentic." Ibid., 142.

106. Raphael R. Abramovitch, "Iu. O. Martov i mirovoi men'shevizm [I. O. Martov and world menshevism]," 73.

107. With apologies to the Tragically Hip, "Ahead by a Century," *Trouble at the Henhouse*, 1996. http://www.thehip.com/albums/Trouble+at+the+Henhouse/.

108. Iulii Martov, *Mirovoi bol'shevizm* [World bolshevism], 11.

109. Grigorii Aronson, *Rossiia v epokhu revoliutsii: Istoricheskie etiudy i memuary* [Russia in the age of the revolution: Historical sketches and

memoirs], 67. The figures for Putilov are taken from S. P. Mel'gunov,
Kak bol'sheviki zakhvatili vlast' [How the bolsheviks seized power].
Paris: La Renaissance, 1953. Available in abridged English translation.
Melgunov, *The Bolshevik Seizure of Power*, 95.

110. Aronson, *Rossiia v epokhu revoliutsii* [Russia in the age of the
revolution], 181; Compare with Grégoire Aronson, "Ouvriers russes
contre le bolchévisme," 201; The chapter of Aronson's book from
which this is taken, is an updated version of an article published
in 1952. Aronson, "Rabochee dvizhenie v bor'be s bol'shevistskoi
diktaturoi" [The labour movement in the struggle against the bolshevik
dictatorship].

I. The Roots of World Bolshevism

1. The Russian original is *gnilogo Zapada*, translated as either "the rotten
West" or the "decaying West," a phrase whose roots are in nineteenth
century disputes between Slavophiles and Westernizers. Arthur Rees
writes that the term refers to "the west of the struggles between the
rulers and the ruled; between Scripture and tradition and the upper and
lower classes." Arthur D. Rees, "An Interpretation of Slavophilism," 52.

2. "International" is shorthand for the Second International (officially
called the Second International Workingmen's Association), formed
in 1889, soon to bring together the principal socialist parties in Europe
and to some extent the rest of the world, effectively ceasing to exist
in August 1914, when most of its constituent parties supported their
respective governments in the First World War. J. C. Docherty, *Historical
Dictionary of Socialism* (hereafter *HDS*), 208–9.

3. It is especially important here not to forget that we are talking about
1918 and early 1919. —*Dan*

   Karl Johann Kautsky (1854–1938) was the principal theorist
of Germany's Social Democratic Party (SPD), the largest and most
influential party within the Second International. After 1917, he became
one of the main socialist critics of Bolshevik Russia. *HDM*, 164-65.

4. The end of the First World War in Germany was marked by a revolution
which saw mutinies by sailors and soldiers, the emergence of councils
(soviets) of workers, soldiers and sailors, and the replacement of the

autocratic Kaiser by what came to be known as the Weimar Republic. Pierre Broué, *The German Revolution, 1917-1923*, 129–260.

5. Russia's revolution in 1917 initially led to independence for many formerly subjugated nations, including Finland. In that country, November 1917 saw a general strike, December 1917 a declaration of independence (recognized by the Bolshevik-led Russian state) and January 1918, the beginning of a civil war between the Finnish Left and the conservative "Whites". A military intervention by Germany proved decisive, leading to the victory of the Whites, and the defeat of the Left. Risto Alapuro, *State and Revolution in Finland*, 137–78.

6. The term "soviet" has acquired a very specific meaning in the years since the Russian Revolution, a meaning implicated with the authoritarianism which developed in what was to become the Soviet Union. In other places—Germany, in particular—while "soviet" is accurate linguistically as a translation of the Russian original, it is often more meaningful in English-language translation to understand this as "council," and this will on occasion be indicated throughout.

7. Hugo Haase (1863-1919) and Friedrich Ebert (1871-1925) were two of the leading socialists in early 20th century Germany. Ebert was part of the conservative pro-war SPD majority, in February 1919 elected president of the new German Republic. Haase before the war emerged as a leading member of the SPD, serving as cochair of the party from 1911 until 1916. The pressures of war ultimately led to a split in the SPD, Haase and others on the antiwar left wing of the party forming the Independent Social Democrats (USPD) in the spring of 1917. In the post-war period Haase and Ebert briefly collaborated. From the November revolution of 1918 until February 1919—i.e., prior to Ebert's election and the consolidation of the Weimar Republic—a coalition of socialist parties was the *de facto* government of Germany. The coalition was dominated by Ebert for the SPD and included Haase from that section of the USPD which agreed to participate in the coalition (many on the left of the USPD were opposed to cooperating with the SPD). Haase was assassinated by a German nationalist in 1919. Broué, *The German Revolution*, 969. HDS, 80-82. David W. Morgan, *The Socialist Left and the German Revolution*, 461.

8. Martov takes this phrase from Pliny the Elder, *Pliny's Natural History, in Thirty-Seven Books*, book 7, p. 174: "Man alone she [Nature] hath cast all

Naked upon the bare Earth, even on his Birth-day, immediately to cry and lament."

9. *Burgfrieden*—literally "truce" or "civil peace," in this context best understood as a "truce between parties"—refers to an agreement, in Germany, during the First World War in Germany, "under which political parties vowed not to compete with each other or challenge the government, which acquired special wartime dictatorial powers." Helen Scott, "Introduction to Rosa Luxemburg," 23.

"Socialization of consciousness" is best understood as "making consciousness operate on socialist principles."

10. Mikhail Alexandrovich Bakunin (1814-1876) was a leading member of the First International (the International Workingmen's Association which preceded the Second or Socialist International), and one of the early figures in European Anarchism. Socialists such as Rosa Luxemburg and Paul Levi challenged Bakunin-influenced politics, disagreeing that a radical minority could "force" a revolution against the wishes of the majority. *HDS*, 34-5; Rosa Luxemburg, "The Mass Strike, the Political Party, and the Trade Union," 111–13; Paul Levi, "Our Path: Against Putschism," 147.

Ferdinand Lassalle (1825-1864) was the founder of the General German Workingmen's Association, often seen as that country's first socialist party, and from its founding in 1863 until 1875 the largest. It became an important component part of the founding of the SPD in 1875. Lassalle focussed on winning reforms with an emphasis on workers' cooperatives. *HDS*, 152. Eduard Bernstein, *Ferdinand Lassalle as a Social Reformer*.

The term "sans-culottes" is widely used as a shorthand for the radical, urban masses of the late eighteenth century French Revolution. During that revolution, the Jacobin leader Maximilien Robespierre used to differentiate the aristocratic elite with their "golden breeches" from the artisans and shopkeepers who did not wear breeches (hence "sans-culottes") but more typically wore long trousers. *HDFR*, 294-5; Albert Soboul, *The Sans-Culottes*, 2.

11. Émile Vandervelde (1866-1938) was a leading member of the Belgian Workers' Party. Supporting Belgium and the Allied Powers in the world war, in 1916 he accepted an invitation to join the war cabinet of the Belgian government.

Philipp Scheidemann (1865-1939) was a German socialist and SPD leader. Supporting Germany and the Central Powers in the world war, in October 1918 he was appointed minister without portfolio in the German wartime government. Scheidemann would in 1919 briefly serve as Chancellor of the new German Republic. Famously, it was Scheidemann in November 1918, who decided to "proclaim the Republic" from a balcony in Berlin, before a demonstration of tens of thousands. Broué, *The German Revolution*, 149. *HDS*, 206, 234–35.

By "laughing third," Martov is referencing the *tertius gaudens* made famous by Georg Simmel. According to Simmel, while there are often two principles in a relationship or a conflict, an often relatively passive "third party" may in the end become the principal beneficiary of their relationship and/or competition. Georg Simmel, "The Triad," in *The Sociology of Georg Simmel*, 145–69.

12. Martov here caught the attention of Lenin, who penned an angry (and unfinished) riposte, directly quoting this first portion of Martov's paragraph, a riposte in which you can feel the emotionally charged differences of that era. Lumping together Martov and Kautsky, Lenin says, "In this reasoning there is so much sophisticated villainy, such an abyss of lies, such deception of the workers, such deep betrayal of their interests, such hypocrisy and abandonment of socialism that you marvel at how much servility Kautsky and Martov have accumulated in the course of decades of 'playing' with opportunism!" V. I. Lenin, "V lakeiskoi" [In the servants' quarters], (July 1919, first published 1925), in *PSS*, 39:143. Compare with *LCW*, 29:543.

13. The Kienthal Conference was a 1916 anti-war gathering, designed to build on the work of the more well-known 1915 anti-war Zimmerwald Conference. In 1919 a resolution at a USPD congress ended with the phrase, "in the spirit of the international conferences in Zimmerwald and Kienthal," a shorthand for anti-war internationalist socialism which would need no translation for activists of that generation. *HDS*, 144. Broué, *The German Revolution*, 337.

14. Georg Wilhelm Friedrich Hegel, "Preface" to *Philosophy of Right*. In Greek mythology, knowledge and understanding were symbolized by the owl of Minerva. Hegel, then, is saying that knowledge and understanding are always clearer at the end of the day—i.e., retrospectively.

15. Here Martov references another core idea from Hegel. According to Robert Pippin, Hegel "divides up the domains of nature and spirit in the same way as Kant, as between the realm of necessity and the realm of freedom, or between events for which causes can be sought (which stand under laws, which laws, together with empirical initial conditions, determine a unique future) and actions for which reasons may be demanded (which are enacted because of conceptions of law')" Robert Pippin, "Hegel's Practical Philosophy," 180.

16. Martov is here making oblique reference to a speech by Lenin in January 1918, where Lenin relayed the following anecdote. "One old Bolshevik gave a correct explanation of Bolshevism to a Cossack. The Cossack asked him: 'Is it true that you Bolsheviks plunder?' 'Yes, indeed,' said the old man, 'we plunder the plunder.'" V. I. Lenin, "Speech to Propagandists [Newspaper Report, *Pravda*, 6 February 1918]," in *LCW*, 26:516.

17. The English Revolution of the 17th century was marked by a civil war between supporters of the monarchy and supporters of Parliament, culminating in the overthrow of the monarchy and the 1649 execution of King Charles I. According to Christopher Hill, "the English Revolution of 1640-60 was a great social movement like the French Revolution of 1789. The state power protecting an old order that was essentially feudal was violently overthrown, power passed into the hands of a new class, and so the freer development of capitalism was made possible." Christopher Hill, *The English Revolution 1640*, 6.

    The late Neil Davidson documented the other side of these revolutions, including the sometimes-arbitrary nature of the 1793-94 Great Terror in France and the brutal war against Ireland carried out by the English revolutionaries. "There are therefore great difficulties involved in ascribing a progressive role to the system responsible for such events." Neil Davidson, *How Revolutionary Were the Bourgeois Revolutions?*, 632–57.

18. The year 1848 witnessed a series of revolutionary upheavals throughout Europe, the most profound of which was in France, culminating in the abdication of the king on 24 February 1848, and the creation of France's short-lived Second Republic. According to Ferdinand Lassalle, "The 24th February 1848 saw the first light of the dawning of a new historical era." Quoted in Eduard Bernstein, *The Preconditions of Socialism*, 136.

    The Second Republic was overthrown in a December 1851 coup

carried out by the republic's own president, Louis-Napoléon Bonaparte (nephew of the famous Napoleon I). Bonaparte would go down in history as "Napoleon III," dictator of France's Second Empire (1852–1870).

19. "Sabotage" refers to the two-month long strike by government employees—a strike movement that spread to teachers, librarians, bank employees, telephone and telegraph operators—in the immediate aftermath of the October overturn in Russia in 1917. Tony Cliff, *Lenin*, vol. 3, *Revolution Besieged*, 15.

20. The Spartacist group (Spartakusbund) whose most prominent figures were Rosa Luxemburg and Karl Liebknecht, originated as the anti-war wing of the SPD in 1914, helped form the USPD in 1917, and would ultimately provide the core of the German Communist Party (KPD) founded early January 1919. According to Broué: "When the Spartacus group, following Liebknecht, declared that the main enemy was at home, it took its place in the revolutionary wing which was gradually taking shape within the international socialist movement." Broué, *The German Revolution*, 64.

21. In our time, Martov could, of course, give still more striking examples of the lack of care for and even conscious destruction of the forces of production by a bourgeois reaction—all while speaking tirelessly of the development and preservation of these same forces of production. Suffice it to recall the devastating damage done by the magnates of capital to the entire national economy of Germany, especially its finances, or the prolonged complete paralysis of Ruhr industry as a result of its occupation under the leadership of French capital. —*Dan*

22. Antoine Laurent Lavoisier (1753-1794) is often regarded as the founder of modern chemistry. One of the many victims of the Terror during the French Revolution, he was executed in May 1794, for having been a tax agent of the former king. It was in fact one of the three judges at his trial who said: "The Republic has no need for scientists." Vivian Grey, *The Chemist Who Lost His Head*, 20.

Maximilien-François-Isidore Robespierre (1758-1794) was the most prominent Jacobin leader during the French Revolution. He was elected to the Committee of Public Safety in July 1793, the executive power of the French government from April 1793 until October 1795. A split in the Jacobins led to his arrest on 9 Thermidor (27 July) 1794, and he was executed the next day, effectively marking the end of the Terror. *HDFR*, 280-82.

Jean-Paul Marat (1743-1793) acquired the nickname "Friend of the People" during the French Revolution, after the name of the paper *L'Ami du Peuple* which he launched in 1789. From 1792, Marat and his paper were supported by the Club of the Cordeliers. On 13 July 1793, he was stabbed to death in his bath by Charlotte Corday. *HDFR*, 209-10.

The Club of the Cordeliers was "founded in April 1790 as the Society of the Friends of the Rights of Man and Citizen" and according to Hanson was "politically more radical than the Jacobin club." It had a "low membership fee" making it accessible to the some of the urban poor. "Women were also welcome at its meetings which generally ranged between 300 and 400 in attendance." On 24 March 1794, the leaders of the Cordeliers fell victim to Robespierre and the Terror, effectively marking the end of the Cordeliers. *HDFR*, 87–88.

Joseph Priestley (1733-1804) is credited with the discovery of oxygen. In England he was "the central figure in the formation of English Unitarianism, and he anticipated many of the viewpoints of Protestant liberalism in general." He was also a materialist philosopher and a partisan of the French Revolution. To escape persecution for his political views, following the outbreak of war between England and France, he and his family emigrated to the United States in 1794. Ira V. Brown, "The Religion of Joseph Priestley," 85–95.

23. A report on the damage caused by Bolshevik artillery to the dome of the Cathedral of St. Basil the Blessed during the October 1917 battles in Moscow prompted the people's commissar of education, A. Lunacharsky, to resign from the government. He withdrew this resignation request, however, after a few days. —*Dan*

Anatoly Vasil'evich Lunacharsky (1875-1933) was a journalist, writer and philosopher, often called the "poet of the revolution." He joined Lenin and the Bolsheviks in 1904, but in the years following launched a rival left-wing group around the paper *Vpered* (Forward). Lunacharsky worked closely with Trotsky and Martov on the anti-war paper best known by its second name *Nashe slovo* (Our word). In 1917, with Trotsky, he joined the Mezhraionka group (Petrograd Interdistrict Committee) before, along with Trotsky and most other "*Mezhraiontsii*", joining the Bolsheviks, serving as People's Commissariat for Enlightenment

(Education) in the Bolshevik government until resigning in the spring of 1929. Larry E. Holmes, "Lunacharskii, Anatolii Vasil'evich," in *MERSH*, 20: 188–94; *HDRR*, 181–84.

24. Romain Rolland (1866-1944) was a major French literary figure (winner of the Nobel Prize for Literature in 1915) and also a fierce critic of world war. "In the period 1917–1919" Rolland "played with the idea of a fraternal organization of intellectuals, an 'intellectual's international' of thinkers who had not capitulated to war propaganda." David James Fisher, *Romain Rolland and the Politics of Intellectual Engagement*, 47.

   Norman Angell (1872–1967) was a British pacifist intellectual, one of those Rolland saw as being part of the "intellectual's international." Just prior to the outbreak of world war, he formed the short-lived Neutrality League. Martin Ceadel, "Angell, Sir (Ralph) Norman [Formerly Ralph Norman Angell Lane] (1872–1967), Peace Campaigner and Author."

25. Martov is here cryptically citing Molière. The portion in square brackets is not in Martov, but is in Molière, and is necessary for the reference to be properly understood. The full extract is: "Vous l'avez voulu, vous l'avez voulu, George Dandin, vous l'avez voulu; cela vous sied fort bien, et vous voilà ajusté comme il faut; vous avez justement ce que vous méritez." Molière, "George Dandin ou le mari confondu," 24 (act I, scene VII).

II. The Ideology of "Sovietism"

1. The expression "four-tails of suffrage" was associated most closely with the Kadets (Constitutional Democrats). Peter Enticott, *The Russian Liberals and the Revolution of 1905*, 39 and 66n22.

2. Martov is here invoking a quotation from the New Testament, "social betrayal" being substituted for "evil." The portion in square brackets is in the Biblical original, but not in Martov. Matthew 3:37 [KJV]).

3. The "sweet and bitter" imagery, used here and elsewhere in this section, is a variation on a traditional Russian proverb: "If you don't taste the bitter, you won't know the sweet." Alexander Margulis and Asya Kholodnaya, *Russian-English Dictionary of Proverbs and Sayings*, 142.

4. Peace negotiations between the new Bolshevik-led state and the German state took place in the German-controlled border town of Brest-Litovsk (today known as Brest, a city in Belarus), following an armistice in December 1917. The Brest-Litovsk treaty was eventually agreed to and

signed by representatives of the Russian state on 3 March 1918, with terms that were extremely punitive toward Russia. "Russia lost its sovereign claims to about 34 percent of its population, 32 percent of its agricultural lands, 85 percent of its sugar beet lands, 54 percent of its industrial establishments and 89 percent of its coal mines." G. Douglas Nicoll, "Brest-Litovsky, Treaty of," in *MERSH*, 20: 188–94.

5. Nikolai Ivanovich Bukharin (1888-1938) was an "Old Bolshevik," a widely published economist and theoretician, and a close associate of Lenin's, who famously called him the "darling of the party." One of the many victims of the Great Terror under Stalin, he was executed in August 1936—belatedly "rehabilitated" in 1988. Lyman H. Legters, "Bukharin, Nikolai Ivanovich," in *MERSH*, 5: 237–40; *HDRR*, 70–72; Lande, "Posthumous Rehabilitation and the Dust-Bin of History," 267.

6. Martov's transcription of this wireless message, while having essentially the same meaning, differs from what we have in the Russian version of Lenin's collected works: "Report, please, what actual guarantees you have that the new Hungarian Government will actually be communist, and not merely socialist, that is composed of social-traitors." V. I. Lenin, "Radiotelegramma Bela Kunu" [Telegram to Béla Kun] (March 1919, first published 1932), in *PSS*, 38:217. Compare with the standard English translation, *LCW*, 29:227. "(!)" appears in Martov's Russian-language version.

   Béla Kun (1886-1939), was an Hungarian conscript soldier in the world war. After being captured by the Russians in 1916, he led a Marxist study circle among other Hungarian prisoners of war, a study circle which became the core of the Hungarian Group of the Russian Communist Party (Bolshevik). In November 1918, he returned to Budapest, was arrested for his political activities, and then in confusing circumstances emerged from jail in March 1919 as the head of the Hungarian Soviet Republic. When the republic collapsed 1 August 1919, Kun sought exile in Russia, where he went on to play a leading role in the Communist International. Arrested during the years of Stalin's Great Terror, he apparently died in prison in 1939. Kun, like many others, was posthumously rehabilitated. James K. Libbey, "Kun, Béla," in *MERSH*, 18: 163–65.

7. While identical in meaning, Martov's Russian version in these two quotations, has wording that is slightly different from that in the

standard Russian edition. See V. I. Lenin, *Gosudarstvo i revoliutsiia* [The
state and revolution], 1917, in *PSS*, 33:109, 42–43. Compare with the
standard English translation, *LCW* 25:486, 424–25.

8. The first quote from Lenin can be found in *The Tasks of the Proletariat in
Our Revolution*, 10 April 1917 (published September 1917); Martov added
the emphasis, as well as the word "universal." The second quotation,
about the election of judges, can be found in Lenin's *Materials Relating
to the Revision of the Party Programme*, April–May 1917 (published June
1917). For the English, see, respectively, *LCW*, 24:70 and 24:473.

9. Arthur Tsutsiev, "Administrative Units of the Russian Empire and the
USSR".

Vladimir Evgenievich Trutovskii (1889-1937), was a leading Left SR,
and commissar in the Bolshevik-Left SR coalition government, until
resigning along with all the Left SRs, in protest at the signing of the
Brest-Litovsk treaty. *HDRR*, 267.

Imprisoned in Moscow in 1923, a group of Left SR prisoners launched
a hunger strike to protest horrendous conditions, in the course of
which Trutovskii attempted to commit suicide by self-immolation.
Abramowitsch [Abramovitch], Suchomlin, and Zeretelli [Tsereteli], *Der
Terror Gegen Die Sozialistischen Parteien in Russland Und Georgien* [The
Terror against Socialist Parties in Russia and Georgia], 41 and 69.

Trutovskii was executed in 1937 during the Great Terror,
posthumously rehabilitated in 1992. https://stalin.memo.ru/persons/
p9101/.

10. Lenin, *Gosudarstvo i revoliutsiia* [The state and revolution], in *PSS*,
33:53. In Martov's Russian original, the wording of the quotation differs
slightly from that in the *PSS* edition, but the meaning is unchanged. For
the standard English translation, see *LCW*, 25:434.

11. V. I. Lenin, *On Slogans*, July 1917, in *LCW*, 25:185–92.

The "July Days" were two days of armed demonstrations in Petrograd,
3 and 4 (16 and 17) July 1917, in the context of a disastrous offensive
launched by the Russian armies in the world war. "For two whole days"
writes Abramovitch, "trucks packed with soldiers, sailors and some
workers, all armed with loaded rifles, roamed up and down" the streets of
the city. Samuel Oppenheim estimates the numbers demonstrating on 4
July as upwards of half a million. David Mandel says that approximately
400 were injured or killed, resulting from "clashes between the

demonstrators and provocateurs." Abramovitch, *The Soviet Revolution: 1917-1939*, 59; Samuel A. Oppenheim, "July Days," in *MERSH*, 15: 150–56; David Mandel, *The Petrograd Workers and the Fall of Old Regime*, 191.

Lenin's pamphlet *On Slogans* clearly makes the claim that "All power to the Soviets!" was a dated slogan, but it does not explicitly make the claim that it should be replaced by the slogan "All power to the Bolshevik Party." Martov may be referencing a Bolshevik Central Committee resolution which in July 1917, in the wake of the July Days, did vote to replace the slogan "All power to the soviets" with that of "All power to the working class led by its revolutionary party—the Bolshevik-Communists." Oppenheim, "July Days," in *MERSH*, 15: 154.

Interestingly, however, in an unpublished and unfinished article where he sharply criticizes many aspects of Martov's analysis, Lenin remains silent on this quite important point. Lenin, "V lakeiskoi" [In the servants' quarters], in *PSS*, 39:139–45. Compare with *LCW*, 29:540–46.

12. Here and throughout, Martov is invoking a phrase made famous by Marx, when he described the Paris Commune of 1871 as "the political form at last discovered under which to work out the economical emancipation of labour." Karl Marx, *The Civil War in France: Address of the General Council of the International Working-Men's Association* (third English edition, August 1871), in *MECW*, 22:333–34.

13. The committees of the poor—often known as "Kombedy", an acronym derived from their Russian name (*komitety bednoty*)—were established by decree on 11 June 1918 and were, according to James Nutsch, "the most significant early feature of War Communism." Through these committees, the poorest peasants were organized and allied with "Bolshevik-backed groups from the city, primarily armed detachments of workers, but at times by members of the Cheka and even Red Army soldiers." In theory, this was a class war against the very rich among the peasantry, but in practice this pitted the poor peasants "against families who often owned not more than a few acres of land and two or three head of cattle." The Kombedy were disbanded by decree 2 December 1918. James G. Nutsch, "Committees of the Poor," in *MERSH*, 7: 210–12.

14. Louis August Blanqui (1805-1881)—labelled by some a communist and revolutionary (Bernstein), by others an "insurrectionist" (Docherty)—was influential in the European left of the nineteenth century and according to Bernstein, "took an active part in all Paris uprisings from

1830 to 1870." Prior to the unsuccessful May 1839 uprising in Paris, Monty Johnstone says that "Blanqui sought to organise a relatively small, centralised, hierarchical elite to prepare and lead an insurrection, which would replace capitalist state power by its own temporary revolutionary dictatorship." Johnstone says that while Marx and Engels came to reject this conception of an "educational dictatorship by a revolutionary minority," they nonetheless held him "in high esteem." During the Paris Commune of 1871, Blanquists were the most influential left current. Bernstein, *The Preconditions of Socialism*, xliii. *HDS*, 107. Monty Johnstone, "Marx, Blanqui and Majority Rule," 299–306.

15. In his well-known speech at the Second Congress of the RSDRP in 1903. —*Dan*

In that speech, Plekhanov said: "Any given democratic principle should be considered not by itself in the abstract, but in its relation to what may be called the basic principle of democracy, namely the principle which says that *salus populi suprema lex* [the welfare of the people is the highest law] .... [I]f, for the sake of the success of the revolution, it was necessary to temporarily restrict the operation of this or that democratic principle, then it would be a crime to refrain from imposing such a restriction. My personal opinion, I will say, is that even the principle of universal suffrage must be looked at from the point of view of what I have called the basic principle of democracy. Hypothetically we can think of a case where we social democrats would be against universal suffrage. ... The revolutionary proletariat may restrict the political rights of the upper classes, just as the upper classes had once restricted their [the proletariat's] political rights. The suitability of such a measure could only be judged in terms of the principle: *salus revolutionis suprema lex* [the welfare of the revolution is the highest law]." Institut Marksizma-Leninizma pri tsk *KPSS* [Institute of Marxism-Leninism of the Central Committee of the CPSU], *Vtoroi s"ezd RSDRP Iiul'-Avgust 1903 Goda: Protokoly* [Second Congress of the RSDLP July-August 1903: Minutes], 181–82.

See note 25 in Section III for Martov's comments on this speech.

16. It is worth recalling here Kautsky's remarks about the "curial" nature of Soviet elections and their inevitable consequences. —*Martov.*

The term "curial" references the limited suffrage allowed under tsarism. Voting eligibility in Russia was expanded after the 1905 revolution but did not by any means amount to universal suffrage. Access to the vote "depended on the ownership of property or the payment of taxes, and the population was divided into four curiae: landowners, peasants, town dwellers, and workers" leading to very skewed representation. Landowners, for instance, comprised 32.7 percent of the electors, while workers comprised just 2.5 per cent. Abraham Ascher, *The Revolution of 1905: A Short History*, 110–11.

Eligibility to vote under the Soviet system was also weighted by economic class location. The 1918 draft Soviet constitution "lays it down that not all the inhabitants of the Russian Empire, but only specified categories have the right to elect deputies to the Soviets. All those may vote who procure their sustenance by useful or productive work." Among those whom this definition excluded was "the worker who loses his work, and endeavours to get a living by opening a small shop, or selling newspapers." Karl Kautsky, *The Dictatorship of the Proletariat*, 81–82.

17. Charles Naine, *Dictature du prolétariat ou démocratie*, 7.

Charles Naine (1874-1926) was a prominent anti-war socialist from Switzerland. He joined the anti-militarist league in 1905, and was a leading figure in the building of the Social Democratic Party (SPS). Karl Lang, "Naine, Charles."

18. V. Vorovskii, later Soviet representative at Rome, killed in Lausanne, May 1923. —*Dan*

19. P. Orlovskii, "Kommunisticheskii Internatsional i Mirovaia Sovetskaia Respublika" [The Communist International and the World Soviet Republic]. Martov gives the date for this article as 13 March 1919, when in fact it was 13 May 1919.

20. Ibid.

Alexander Feodorovich Kerensky (1881-1970) was a prominent leader of the Russian progressive movement, associated variously with the Social-Revolutionaries and the Trudovik Party (a small agrarian socialist party, close to the Constitutional Democrats). As minister of justice following the February (March) Revolution of 1917, Docherty listed his main accomplishments as "abolishing ethnic and religious discrimination—a czarist policy that particularly affected Jews—and the death penalty." Kerensky served as Prime Minister until the Bolshevik seizure of power in October (November) 1917. *HDS*, 143-44. *HDRR*, 152-56.

21. Translated directly from Martov. "(!)" appears in the Russian text.
22. After the split of the Independent Party [USPD] at the congress of 1920 in Halle, he moved to the Communists. —*Dan*

    Ernst Däumig (1866-1922) was an army veteran who joined the SPD in 1898. During Germany's November 1918 revolution he was one of the leaders of the Revolutionary Shop Stewards' movement in Berlin. He and many others on the Left of the Independent Social Democratic Party (hence "Left Independent") joined the KPD in 1920. Stefan Berger, "Däumig, Ernst."
23. Translated directly from Martov. The original Russian word *filisterskii* has been translated as "pedestrian," here and throughout.

    Fritz Heckert (1884-1936) was born in Chemnitz, Germany, joined the SPD in 1902, and in 1916 co-founded the Chemnitz Group of the Spartacus League (Spartakusbund). A workers' council leader in 1918, he helped co-found the KPD at the end of that year. Klaus Schönhoven, "Heckert, Fritz."
24. Iraklii Georgievich Tsereteli (1881-1959) was a socialist from Georgia, who became a leader of the Menshevik wing of the RSDRP. During the world war he took an internationalist (anti-war) position. When he returned from internal exile after the February / March Revolution of 1917, he played a leading role in the Petrograd Soviet, where he advocated a defensist position (i.e., justifying a continuation of the war in order to defend the revolution). After the dissolution of the Constituent Assembly in January 1918, Tsereteli escaped arrest and returned to Georgia, after the Russian conquest of Georgia, ending up in exile in Europe and eventually the United States. Ziva Galili y Garcia, "Tsereteli, Iraklii Georgievich," in *MERSH*, 40: 25–28.

    Tsereteli co-authored one of the first major exposés of the Russian labour camp system. Abramowitsch [Abramovitch], Suchomlin, and Zeretelli [Tsereteli], *Der Terror Gegen Die Sozialistischen Parteien in Russland Und* Georgien [The Terror against Socialist Parties in Russia and Georgia].
25. See note 11 this section.
26. Martov here makes cryptic, and incomplete reference to a famous phrase from Schiller. The word "servant" is not in the original but preserves the meaning. The portion in square brackets is not in Martov, but is in

Schiller, and is necessary for the reference to be properly understood. Friedrich Schiller, "Fiesco; or, the Genoese Conspiracy," 224.

27. François Noel (Gracchus) Babeuf (1760-1797) in the early years of the French Revolution, published the *Correspondent Picard*, and organized opposition to seigneurial dues. After the overthrow of Robespierre in 1794, he launched the newspaper *Tribun du people*, and later organized an early communist organization, the Conspiracy of Equals. *HDFR*, 23-24.

    Philippe Buonarroti (1761-1837) is primarily known for his book *Buonarroti's History of Babeuf's Conspiracy for Equality* (translated by Bronterre. 1836. London: H. Hetherington.) He was also "in the front ranks among the conspirators who, prior to 1859, worked for the liberation of Italy." Georges Weill, "Philippe Buonarroti (1761-1837)," 241.

28. The standard English-language translation is slightly different. "All Socialists with the exception of the followers of Fourier ... are agreed that the form of government which is called the sovereignty of the people is a very unsuitable, and even dangerous, sheet anchor for the young principle of Communism about to be realized." Quoted in Kautsky, *The Dictatorship of the Proletariat*, 20.

    Wilhelm Weitling (1808-1871) was one of many German veterans of the 1848 revolution, who after the revolution, emigrated to the United States of America. Hans Mühlestein calls him "the most important proletarian representative of 'equalitarian communism.'" Carl Frederick Wittke, *The Utopian Communist; a Biography of Wilhelm Weitling, Nineteenth-Century Reformer*, v. Hans Mühlestein, "Marx and the Utopian Wilhelm Weitling," 113.

    François Marie Charles Fourier (1772-1837) was a French utopian socialist. "He envisaged a harmonious society based on cooperative communities that he called *phalanstères*, (phalanxes)." *HDS*, 91. According to Bernstein, during the French Revolution, he "survived the 'Terror' by the skin of his teeth." Bernstein, *The Preconditions of Socialism*, xliv.

29. Étienne Cabet (1788-1856) was one of a group of thinkers labelled "utopian socialist" by Marx and Engels because of their "visionary schemes for separate societies practicing social equality." *HDS*, 233.

30. Georges Bourgin and Hubert Bourgin, *Le socialisme français de 1789 à 1848*, 64–65.

Armand Barbes (1809–1870) was a French revolutionary democrat and associate of Blanqui. Bernstein, *The Preconditions of Socialism*, xlii–xliii.

31. Émile Pouget, La Confédération générale du travail, 34–35.

Émile Pouget (1860-1931) was "one of the founders and leaders of revolutionary trade-unionism in France." Edward Peter Fitzgerald, "Emile Pouget, the Anarchist Movement, and the Origins of Revolutionary Trade-Unionism in France (1880-1901)," i.

32. Robert Owen (1771-1858) born in Montgomeryshire Britain, was a well-to-do philanthropist and later in life, a socialist. He was famous for purchasing the community of New Harmony, Indiana, to set up a "model" community. Owen was one of the most well-known of those often labelled "utopian socialist." *HDS*, 187-88; Gregory Claeys, "Owen, Robert (1771-1858), Socialist and Philanthropist."

33. In deploying the phrase "of blessed memory," Martov was signalling a political, not actual, obituary for Gustave Hervé (1871-1944). Two years prior to the outbreak of world war, Hervé abandoned his previous anti-war radicalism, and came out as a French patriot, after the war becoming an infamous far right "national socialist," going so far as to argue "that France needed its own version of Hitler or Mussolini." Michael B. Loughlin, "Gustave Hervé's Transition from Socialism to National Socialism," 531.

34. While this idea is very much part of the Owen text, I could not find this direct quotation as presented by Martov. Robert Owen, *A New View of Society and Other Writings*.

35. Karl Marx, "Marx über Feuerbach" [Theses on Feuerbach], 793. This translation is my own, and differs from the standard English one in certain respects, including by substituting "people" for "man," "education" for "upbringing," and "educators" for "educator," the latter to facilitate use of the third-person pronoun. The emphasis on "above" was added by Martov. Compare with *MECW*, 5:7.

36. The possibility for the proletariat to achieve complete spiritual emancipation in bourgeois society was the subject of lively debates in the Menshevik literature on the eve of the war (in articles by Potresov, Martynov Cherevanin et al. in *Nasha zaria* [Our dawn]), and even earlier in the emigrant literature in articles by A. Bogdanov, A. Lunacharsky et al.). —*Martov*

37. The suppression of all press except the official one has its supporters and has even been partially tried in the West under the sweet-sounding name "socialization of the press." —*Martov*

III. Decomposition or Conquest of the State?

1. A mass movement in Britain in the 1830s and 1840s, Chartism—"named after the People's Charter, the statement of its demands"—was in its origins a social movement for democratic reform. "The objectives of the movement were the suffrage for all adult males, annual parliaments, vote by secret ballot, public payment of members of parliament, population equality of electoral districts, and the abolition of property qualifications for members of parliament." *HDS*, 57-58.

   The Chartists were also early precursors of organized labour and collective labour action, the August 1842 general strike they organized and led posing "a profound challenge to early industrial capitalism." Mark O'Brien, *Perish the Privileged Orders: A Socialist History of the Chartist Movement*, 38.

   James Elishama Smith (1801-1857) was born near Glasgow in Scotland. John Saville describes him as "editor of the weekly *Crisis*, the main Owenite journal, from the autumn of 1833 until its demise in August 1834." Timothy Stunt suggests that he is the person behind the pseudonym Senex, who in 1834, wrote "a series of '*Letters on associated labour*' in James Morrison's *Pioneer*." Saville, "JE Smith and the Owenite Movement, 1833-1834," 115; Timothy C. F. Stunt, "Smith, James Elishama [Called Shepherd Smith]."

   James Morrison (1802-1835), born in Newcastle upon Tyne in Britain, was a follower of Robert Owen. In 1832 he launched a weekly newspaper, *The Pioneer*. When Morrison became a member of the executive of the Grand National Consolidated Trades Union (GNCTU) in 1834, *The Pioneer* became that organization's newspaper, the "circulation of which at its peak may have reached 30,000 copies." John Rule, "Morrison, James (1802–1835), Journalist and Trade Unionist."

2. Quoted in Max Beer, *A History of British Socialism*, 339. The Russian version, cited by Martov, uses the phrase "trade-union" or "trades-unions" where, in every instance, Beer in the English original simply says "trade"

or "trades." The Russian version renders "not easily recovered" as "will never be recovered."

3. Quoted in Beer, 340. The emphasis throughout is Martov's.

4. Quoted in Ibid., 337. The emphasis is Martov's.

   Bronterre O'Brien (James O'Brien, 1804-1864), born in Ireland, would become, shortly after moving to London in 1830, the effective editor of the *Poor Man's Guardian*. "From the beginning of the Chartist movement O'Brien was one of its most prominent figures." Miles Taylor, "O'Brien, James [Pseud. Bronterre O'Brien] (1804–1864), Chartist."

5. Karl Marx and Frederick Engels, *Manifesto of the Communist Party* (English edition of 1888; originally published in German, 1848), in *MECW*, 6:504.

6. Lenin, *The State and Revolution*, 1917, in *LCW*, 25:411.

7. Karl Marx, *The Eighteenth Brumaire of Louis Bonaparte* (edition of 1869; originally published 1852), in *MECW*, 11:186. The words "[previous]" and "[state]" were added in the present translation, for the sake of clarity.

8. Karl Marx, "Letter to Ludwig Kugelmann" (12 April 1871), in *MECW*, 44:131.

   Ludwig Kugelmann (1828-1902) was a "German physician, member of the First International, with whom Marx maintained a lively correspondence for a dozen years (1862-74)." Saul K. Padover, note, in Karl Marx, *On History and People*, ed. Saul K. Padover, 216.

9. Marx, *The Civil War in France*, in *MECW*, 22:331.

10. In *The Civil War in France*, Marx writes, "The Commune was to be a working, not a parliamentary, body, executive and legislative at the same time" (*MECW*, 22:331). It is thus Martov, not Marx, who counterposes "talking" to "working."

11. Marx and Engels, *Manifesto of the Communist Party*, *MECW*, 6:504.

12. Marx, Letter to Kugelmann (*MECW*, 44:131).

13. Aleksandr Herzen, "Letter Ten (Paris, 10 June 1848)," 148.

    Alexander Herzen (1812-1887) was an early Russian socialist and a supporter of Proudhon. *HDS*, 198.

14. Lenin, *Gosudarstvo i revoliutsiia* [The state and revolution], in *PSS*, 33:38. Compare with *LCW*, 25:420. The standard English language translation uses "Britain" instead of "England." The phrase "the prior condition" is not in Martov's version.

15. Lenin, *Gosudarstvo i revoliutsiia* [The state and revolution], in *PSS*, 33:38; emphasis in the original. Compare with *LCW*, 25:421.

16. Frederick Engels, *Anti-Dühring: Herr Eugen Dühring's Revolution in Science*, 1894, in *MECW*, 25:268.

17. Frederick Engels, "Introduction," to the third German edition (1891) of Karl Marx, *The Civil War in France*, in *MECW*, 27:190.

18. Frederick Engels, "A Critique of the Draft Social-Democratic Programme of 1891" (29 June 1891, first published 1901–2), in *MECW*, 27:227. Emphasis added by Martov.

19. "The Erfurt Program was the official policy of the German Social Democratic Party adopted at the party's conference at Erfurt in October 1891." *HDS*, 85.

20. Lenin, *Gosudarstvo i revoliutsiia* [The state and revolution], in *PSS*, 33:70–71. Compare with *LCW*, 25:450.

21. But, of course, Engels does not go as far as the current leader of the German Communist Party, Brandler, who stated during his trial that the dictatorship of the proletariat can be realized in Germany without changing its current constitution. —*Dan*

22. Engels, "Introduction," in *MECW*, 27:190.

23. Kautsky, *The Dictatorship of the Proletariat*, 43. Martov's quote does not include the last part of Kautsky's statement, "which must everywhere arise when the proletariat has conquered political power." It is included here, because without it the sentence becomes difficult to understand.

24. Marx, *The Civil War in France*, in *MECW*, 22:336. The words in square brackets have been added to make this English-translation consistent with the Russian-language version used by Martov.

25. In 1903, as is well known, G. V. Plekhanov declared that when the revolutionary proletariat has realized its dictatorship, it may find it necessary to deprive the bourgeoisie of all political rights (including the right to vote). However, for Plekhanov this was one of the *possibilities* of the dictatorship of the proletariat, and not necessarily its inevitable consequence. In my pamphlet *The Struggle against the State of Siege within the Social-Democratic Labor Party of Russia*, I tried to interpret Plekhanov's words as presenting an example *admissible only in logical* abstraction and therefore used by him to illustrate the thesis "the welfare of the revolution is the highest law," to which all other considerations must be subordinated. I expressed the belief that Plekhanov himself

probably did not presume that the proletariat of countries that were economically ripe for socialism would, upon acquiring power, find themselves in a situation where it was not possible for them to support themselves on the willing acceptance of their direction by the people but, on the contrary, had to deny to the bourgeois minority, by force, the exercise of political rights. In a private conversation with me, Plekhanov expressed displeasure with this interpretation of his words. I understood then that his concept of the dictatorship of the proletariat was not devoid of the features characteristic of the *Jacobin dictatorship by a revolutionary minority.* —*Martov.*

26. During the French Revolution: "The Montagnards were the left-wing deputies in the National Convention" which sat from 20 September 1792 until 26 October 1795, "and represented one of the two main political factions within that body, the other being the Girondins." The label "Montagnard" was coined by Joseph-Marie Lequinio, labelling these left-wingers the "deputies of the Mountain (*la Montagne*)" in the Legislative Assembly which sat from 1 October 1791 until 20 September 1792, "because they chose to sit in the highest seats of the meeting hall." *HDFR,* 223.

    It was also in the Legislative Assembly that the Girondins "first become recognizable" as a distinct political current. During the trial of the former king, Louis XVI, they were denounced by the Montagnards for allegedly trying to save him from execution. Following the insurrection of 31 May 1793, many Girondins were proscribed from sitting in the National Convention. Any who remained in Paris were executed. Many of those who fled were eventually captured and "either committed suicide or died on the guillotine." *HDFR,* 140–42.

27. Paul Louis, historian of French socialism, writes: "The 18th of March took on the aspect of a rebellion of Paris against provincial oppression." —*Martov.*

    In the source he cites for this quotation, the nearest equivalent I could find was the following: "The May 1871 crushing [of the Paris Commune] can be explained, in large part, by the antagonism and moral divide between Paris and the provinces." Paul Louis, *Histoire du socialisme français,* 304.

28. James Guillaume, *L'Internationale: Documents et souvenirs (1864–1878),* 2:133.

29. Martov is in fact referencing a letter to Sorge in which Marx does say he "defended them" but says nothing about "honour." Karl Marx, "Marx to Friedrich Adolph Sorge" (9 November 1871), in *MECW*, 44:241–42.

30. Pierre-Joseph Proudhon (1809-1865) was a French radical active in the Revolution of 1848. Proudhon in 1840, according to Merriman, was "the first to call himself an anarchist." Docherty reminds us that Proudhon "became famous for his declaration that 'property is theft.'" Johnston says that the Proudhonists, after the Blanquists, were the second most influential left current during the Paris Commune of 1871. John M. Merriman, *The Dynamite Club: How a Bombing in Fin-de-Siècle Paris Ignited the Age of Modern Terror*, 42. *HDS*, 198. Johnstone, "Marx, Blanqui and Majority Rule," 306.

    Jacques René Hébert (1757-1794) was an activist in the Paris Club of the Cordeliers during the French Revolution, editor of *Le Père Duchesne* "which would become one of the most popular, and most maligned, revolutionary newspapers of the capital," a paper which was "written in the language of the people" and would become "the mouthpiece of the Parisian *sans-culottes*." An advocate of the Terror, he eventually became its victim, executed on the guillotine 24 March 1794. *HDFR*, 255.

31. The Russian-language word—*golyt'bu*—which Martov puts in quotations marks here (and to which Dan refers in his introduction) might be translated as "rabble," but that carries with it a quite negative connotation. Given the literature on the French Revolution, we were tempted to use "sans-culottes." However, there is a specific Russian word used throughout the text— *sankiuloty*—with precisely that meaning. In the French language literature, there is another specific term frequently used, *menu people* (little people), which some might suggest as an alternative. HDFR, 294.

32. From the Commune in Paris of Hébert as well as its counterpart in Lyon came the initiative for the extreme measures of political terror (the September executions, the expulsion of the Girondins from the Convention) and also for those socio-revolutionary measures of "consumer communism" by which the impoverished cities attempted to force the petite bourgeoisie of the villages and the outlying provinces to provide them with foodstuffs. It is in the Communes of Paris and Lyon where the expeditions of the *provisioning armies* [i.e., food armies] started. It is there where "committees of poor peasants" were organized

for the purpose of appropriating grain from the so-called "kulaks"—who, in the jargon of the period, were called "aristocrats." The two Communes of the French Revolution extracted contributions from the bourgeoisie and took charge of the stocks of commodities produced by industry during the preceding years (especially at Lyon). From these organizations emanated the requisitioning of residences, the forcible attempts to lodge the poor in houses considered too large for their occupants, and other egalitarian measures. If, in their quest for historical analogies, Lenin, Trotsky, and Radek had shown a greater knowledge of the past, and a lesser inclination to skim over the surface of phenomena, they would not have tried to tie the genealogy of the Soviets to the Commune of 1871, but rather to the Paris Commune of 1793–94, which was a centre of revolutionary energy and power of the strata of the population most similar to the modern proletariat. *—Martov*

Karl Radek (né Sobelsohn, 1885–1939), was born in Lviv (Lvov) in Austrian-occupied Poland and became a prominent figure in the socialist movements of both Poland and Russia. He attended the 1915 Zimmerwald anti-war conference, and from 1917 on worked closely with Lenin. In the early 1920s he played a leading role in the Communist International. Until "capitulating" in 1929, he was a key supporter of Trotsky in the fight against Stalin. Arrested in 1936, and "convicted" in a Show Trial in 1937, he died in a forced labour camp in 1939. Radek was posthumously rehabilitated in 1988. Robert D. Warth, "Radek, Karl," in *MERSH*, 30: 139–43. Lande, "Posthumous Rehabilitation and the Dust-Bin of History," 267.

33. In his letter to Marx, 6 July 1869 [Frederick Engels, "Engels to Marx" (6 July 1869), in *MECW*, 42:308], Engels mentions Tridon's pamphlet *Gironde et Girondins. La Gironde en 1869 et en 1793*, in which the author presents the arguments of that wing of Blanquism: "It's a comic idea that the dictatorship of Paris over France, which led to the *downfall of the first revolution*, could be accomplished without more ado today once again, and with a quite different result." *—Martov*

34. Claude Ovtcharenko, ed., "Déclaration au people français," 903.

35. Arthur Arnould, *Histoire populaire et parlementaire de la Commune de Paris*, 2:142, 144. Except where indicated, emphasis in extracts from Arnould are in the original, but not in Martov's translation.

36. Ibid., 2:147.

37. Georges Sorel (1847–1922) and his follower and co-thinker Édouard Berth (1875–1939) were two of the pre-eminent representatives of the trend of syndicalism (or revolutionary syndicalism) which emerged in France in the late nineteenth and early twentieth century. Syndicalists saw "governments and political parties, including socialist parties, as instruments of working-class oppression. Syndicalist thought stressed direct action, particularly the general strike." J. C. Docherty and Jacobus Hermanus Antonius van der Velden, *Historical Dictionary of Organized Labor* (hereafter *HDOL*), 255.

   At a formal level, Martov is not wrong to include Daniel De Leon (1852-1914) in the same category as Sorel and Berth. De Leon was one of the founders in the United States of the Industrial Workers of the World (IWW or Wobblies), and the IWW has been called "the American expression of syndicalism" *HDOL*, 137.

   However, Sorel and Berth became drawn towards nationalism, and that combined with their rejection of parliamentary democracy and embrace of violence as a means for social change, made their ideas very compatible with fascism. The Wobblies, by contrast, were harsh critics of nationalism. Antonio Gramsci, the Italian Communist leader who would spend years in a fascist jail, took his inspiration from De Leon. Benito Mussolini – the fascist leader of Gramsci's Italy – saw his politics as compatible with those of Sorel. Antonio Gramsci, "On the L'Ordine Nuovo Programme," 296; James H. Meisel, "A Premature Fascist?," 14.

38. Arnould, *Histoire populaire et parlementaire de la Commune de Paris*, 2:147n. Emphasis is Martov's.

39. Ibid., 2:154.

40. Charles Seignobos, "La troisième république."

41. Mitch Abidor, trans., "International Workingmen's Association Federal Council of Parisian Sections."

42. Peter Lavrov, *Parizhskaia kommuna 18 marta 1871 goda* [The Paris Commune of 18 March 1871], 130, 157.

43. Ibid., 156-57.

44. We find today (1918–19) among the Bolsheviks inside and outside Russia the same confusion introduced by the communards with their specific "political form at last discovered" for the social emancipation of the proletariat. They, too, have substituted the territorial organization of the state for the union of producers that, at first, was seen as the essence

of the soviet republic. This substitution is presented to us either as the natural result of the functioning of a fully formed socialist society, or is transformed into a necessary precondition for the accomplishment of the social transformation itself. The confusion becomes hopeless when an attempt is made to overcome it by resorting to the notion of a "soviet state" which is supposed to be the organized violence of the proletariat and, as such, is preparing the ground for the "extinction" of all forms of the state, but which at the same time is itself something fundamentally opposed to the state as such. The Parisian Communards reasoned the same way. They permitted themselves to imagine that the commune-state of 1871 was something whose very principle was the opposite of any form of the state, while, in reality, it represented a simplified modern democratic state functioning in the manner of the Swiss canton. — *Martov*

45. Quoted in Lavrov, *Parizhskaia kommuna 18 marta 1871 goda* [The Paris Commune of 18 March 1871], 158.

46. Karl Marx, "Marx to Engels" (20 June 1866), in *MECW*, 42:287.

47. Marx, *The Civil War in France*, in *MECW*, 22:333–34

48. Ibid.

49. Ibid., 333.

50. Ibid., 334. The italicized portion in the Russian-language version provided by Martov, would translate more literally as "*which is now becoming redundant.*"

51. Ibid., 328.

52. Guillaume, *L'Internationale: Documents et souvenirs (1864–1878)*, 2:191.

53. Martov does not provide a source for this quotation, but Franz Mehring makes a similar point without quoting Bakunin directly. Franz Mehring, *Karl Marx*, 453.

54. Lenin, *The State and Revolution*, in *LCW*, 25:437.

55. Bernstein, *The Preconditions of Socialism*, 154.

     Eduard Bernstein (1850–1932), was one of the most prominent socialists in Germany after the death of Marx and Engels. Challenged by Rosa Luxemburg and others on what she and others called his "revisionism." As an SPD member of the Reichstag, he refused to vote for war credits in 1914. Joined the USPD in 1917, but returned to the SPD in 1918. *HDS*, 40-42.

56. Lenin, *The State and Revolution*, in *LCW*, 25:433–34.

57. Of course, Lenin, too, wrote a great deal on the subject of Eduard Bernstein's book without taking the trouble of correcting that "distortion." —*Martov*

58. "The Address" is shorthand for *The Civil War in France: Address of the General Council of the International Working-Men's Association.*

59. Mehring, *Karl Marx*, 452–53.

60. Ibid., 453.

61. Ibid.

62. Let us recall that Lenin said that if 200,000 landowners could administer an immense territory in their own interests, 200,000 Bolsheviks would do the same thing in the interest of the workers and peasants. —*Martov*

The full quotation from Lenin uses slightly different figures. "Since the 1905 revolution, Russia has been governed by 130,000 landowners, who have perpetrated endless violence against 150,000,000 people, heaped unconstrained abuse upon them, and condemned the vast majority to inhuman toil and semi-starvation.

"Yet we are told that the 240,000 members of the Bolshevik Party will not be able to govern Russia, govern her in the interests of the poor and against the rich. These 240,000 are already backed by no less than a million votes of the adult population, for this is precisely the proportion between the number of Party members and the number of votes cast for the Party that has been established by the experience of Europe and the experience of Russia as shown, for example, by the elections to the Petrograd City Council last August. We therefore already have a 'state apparatus' of *one million* people devoted to the socialist state for the sake of high ideals and not for the sake of a fat sum received on the 20th of every month." V. I. Lenin, "Can the Bolsheviks Retain State Power?," *Prosveshchenie*, nos. 1–2 (1 October 1917), in *LCW*, 26:111.

63. In Iu. O. Martov's papers we found the following alternative lines [after this first comma]:

... the edifice of communalist ideology, surpassed by the development of the labour movement since the time of 1871, is again emerging. This ideology, as in the Paris Commune, combines two tendencies. On the one hand—thanks to the war-induced collapse of socialism and the inner cohesion and organization that is necessary to master the state machine as a whole—the masses try to solve the problem of how to destroy the bourgeoisie's political power by entrenching themselves in autonomous and self-organized urban communes. Like the Paris workers of 1871, the Berlin, Leipzig, Munich, Zurich, or Stockholm communist-minded workers of 1919 do not ask themselves whether the *consistent* implementation of the principle of "All power to the soviets!" will dig a political abyss between town and country, between the industrial centres and petit-bourgeois provinces—an abyss that renders inconceivable the implementation of a unified collectivist economy.

On the other hand, the same masses, overestimating the actual cohesion of the large centres and not realizing the power and significance of all the social forces that they have to deal with during the revolution, are easily inclined toward the idea of the dictatorship of these centres over the whole country, to a "Hébertist" dictatorship of the communes of the major urban centres over the whole country.

Max Adler was absolutely right when, in one of his articles on the problems of the social revolution (in the *Vienna Workers' Journal*), he concluded that "it is sufficient that just one large section of the peasantry stand aside from the socialist movement for us to conclude: the slogan of Soviet government means either naked violence against the peasants or a coalition with the peasants."

Here this alternative breaks off. —Dan

Appendix: Marx and the Problem of the Dictatorship of the Proletariat

1. Rosa Luxemburg, "Social Reform or Revolution," 157.

    Rosa Luxemburg (1870-1919), was the outstanding pre-world war representative of the European internationalist anti-war left. Born in Russian-occupied Poland, she played a leading role in the socialist movement of both countries. Luxemburg famously challenged the "revisionism" of Eduard Bernstein. She was jailed during the world war for her anti-war politics, from jail wrote a devastatingly accurate pamphlet outlining both the strengths and weaknesses of the new Russian state (Luxemburg, "The Russian Revolution."). She helped found the KPD at the end of 1918, and was assassinated just a few days later, in January 1919, by right-wing former army officers. *HDS*, 160-61. Luxemburg, "The Russian Revolution".

2. *Democracy and Dictatorship* is in fact the name of a short book published in Berlin in 1918 that comprises the first half of Kautsky's *The Dictatorship of the Proletariat*, however no such comment appears in that work. Martov is perhaps referring here to an earlier work by Kautsky, *The Road to Power*, where he writes, "In their recognition of the necessity of capturing political power Marx and Engels agreed with Blanqui. But while Blanqui thought it possible to capture the power of the state by a sudden act of a conspiratory minority, and to use that power in the interest of the proletariat, Marx and Engels recognized that revolutions are not made at will" (6).

3. Engels, "Introduction," in *MECW*, 27:520. Martov's emphasis.

4. Ibid., 27: 520.

5. In the authoritative English edition of Marx and Engels's *Collected Works*, this is translated as "The realization of communism is now out of the question. First the bourgeoisie must take the helm." "Notes," in *MECW*, 48:570.

6. The available English translation of the letter puts this as "Marx and Engels argued vehemently against me." Wilhelm Weitling, "Letter by Wilhelm Weitling to Moses Hess."

7. Marx, "Moralising Criticism and Critical Morality" (28 October 1847), in *MECW*, 11:319. Martov's emphasis.

8. Ibid.

9. It was "conservatives who generally referred to the revolution as the 'mad year' or 'crazy year.'" Dieter Langewiesche, "Revolution in Germany: Constitutional State—Nation State—Social Reform," 135.

10. Marx, "The Eighteenth Brumaire of Louis Bonaparte," in *MECW*, 11:191.

11. Compare with the standard English translation: Marx, *The Civil War in France*, in *MECW* 22:336–37. Among the differences with the Russian text used by Martov is the use of the phrase "middle class." We have kept the phrase "Third Estate" used in Martov's Russian text.

12. Karl Marx, "Contribution to the Critique of Hegel's Philosophy of Law. Introduction," (1844), in *MECW*, 3:185. Martov uses "class" instead of "estate," and writes "as early as 1845" rather than 1844.

13. Compare with the standard English translation: Marx, *The Civil War in France*, in *MECW*, 22:338.

14. Engels, "Introduction," in *MECW*, 27:514.

15. Marx, *The Civil War in France*, in *MECW*, 22:338. Martov's emphasis.

16. Ibid., 331–33.

17. Frederick Engels, *Principles of Communism* (October 1847, first published 1914), in *MECW*, 6:350.

18. Marx and Engels, *Manifesto of the Communist Party* (1848), in *MECW*, 6:504.

Bibliography

Abidor, Mitch, trans. "International Workingmen's Association Federal Council of Parisian Sections," 2006. Documents of the Paris Commune. https://www.marxists.org/history/france/paris-commune/documents/international.htm.

[Abramovitch, Raphael R.] *Bolshevik Terror Against Socialists: Documents and Facts Collected by Authority of the Socialist Labor International.* Translated by International Committee for Political Prisoners. New York: Committee for Political Prisoners in Russia, 1925.

Abramovitch, Raphael R. "Iu. O. Martov i mirovoi men'shevizm" [I. O. Martov and world menshevism]. In *Martov i ego blizkie: Sbornik* [Martov and his circle: a Compilation], edited by G. Y. Aronson, L. O. Dan, B.L. Dvinov, and B. M. Sapir, 71-85. New York: s.n., 1959.

———. *The Soviet Revolution, 1917–1939.* Translated by Vera Broido-Cohn and Jacob Shapiro. London: George Allen and Unwin, 1962.

Abramowitsch [Abramovitch], Raphael, Vassily Suchomlin, and Iraklii Zeretelli [Tsereteli]. *Der Terror Gegen Die Sozialistischen Parteien in Russland Und Georgien* [The Terror against Socialist Parties in Russia and Georgia]. Berlin: JHW Dietz Nachfolger, 1925.

Alapuro, Risto. *State and Revolution in Finland.* Historical Materialism Book Series, 174. Leiden: Brill, 2018

Applebaum, Anne. *Gulag: A History.* New York: Random House, 2003.

Arnould, Arthur. *Histoire populaire et parlementaire de la Commune de Paris.* 2 vols. Bruxelles: Librairie Socialiste de Henri Kistemaeckers, 1878.

Aronson, Grégoire. "Ouvriers russes contre le bolchévisme." *Le contrat social* 10, no. 4 (1966): 201–11.

Aronson, Grigorii. "Rabochee dvizhenie v bor'be s bol'shevistskoi diktaturoi" [The Labour movement in the struggle against the bolshevik dictatorship]. *Protiv techeniia: Sbornik* [Against the current: A Collection], 66–77. New York: Waldon Press, 1952.

———. *Rossiia v epokhu revoliutsii: Istoricheskie etiudy i memuary* [Russia in the age of the revolution: Historical sketches and memoirs]. New York: Waldon Press, 1966.

Ascher, Abraham. *The Revolution of 1905: A Short History.* Stanford: Stanford University Press, 2004.

———. *The Revolution of 1905: Russia in Disarray.* Vol. 1. 2 vols. Stanford: Stanford University Press, 1994.

Ascher, Abraham, ed. *The Mensheviks in the Russian Revolution.* Original documents translated by Paul Stevenson. London: Thames and Hudson, 1976.

Axelrod, Pavel Borisovich. "Ob'edinenie rossiiskoi sotsial-demokratii i ee zadachi," [The Unification of Russian social democracy and its tasks]. *Iskra*, no. 55 (15 December 1903) and *Iskra*, no. 57 (15 January 1904).

Bakan, Abigail B. "Marxism, Feminism, and Epistemological Dissonance." *Socialist Studies/Études socialistes* 8, no. 2 (6 December 2012): 60–84.

Beer, Max. *A History of British Socialism.* One volume edition. 1919. Reprint, London: George Allen and Unwin, 1940.

Berger, Stefan. "Däumig, Ernst." In *Biographical Dictionary of European Labor Leaders*, edited by A. T. Lane, 1:245-6. Westport: Greenwood Publishing Group, 1995.

Bernstein, Eduard. *Ferdinand Lassalle as a Social Reformer.* Translated by Eleanor Marx Aveling. New York: Charles Scribner's Sons, 1893.

———. *The Preconditions of Socialism.* Edited and translated by Henry Tudor. 1899. Reprint, Cambridge: Cambridge University Press, 1993.

Bethencourt, Francisco. "The *Auto da Fé*: Ritual and Imagery." *Journal of the Warburg and Courtauld Institutes*, no. 55 (1992): 155–68.

Bourgin, Georges, and Hubert Bourgin. *Le socialisme français de 1789 à 1848.* Paris: Hachette, 1912.

Broué, Pierre. *The German Revolution, 1917-1923.* (1971). Edited by Ian Birchall and Brian Pearce. Translated by John Archer. Historical Materialism Book Series, 5. Leiden: Brill, 2005.

Brown, Ira V. "The Religion of Joseph Priestley." *Pennsylvania History: A Journal of Mid-Atlantic Studies*, 1957, 85–100.

Burbank, Jane. *Intelligentsia and Revolution: Russian Views of Bolshevism, 1917–1922*. New York: Oxford University Press, 1989.

Casey, Jane Barnes. *I, Krupskaya: My Life with Lenin. A Novel*. Boston: Houghton Mifflin, 1974.

Ceadel, Martin. "Angell, Sir (Ralph) Norman [Formerly Ralph Norman Angell Lane] (1872–1967), Peace Campaigner and Author." In *Oxford Dictionary of National Biography*, edited by David Cannadine. Oxford: Oxford University Press, 2004. https://doi.org/10.1093/ref:odnb/30419.

Central Committee of the Russian Social Democratic Workers' Party (United). "Suppression of the Press." 1917. Translated by Paul Stevenson. In *The Mensheviks in the Russian Revolution*, edited by Abraham Ascher, 107–8. London: Thames and Hudson, 1976.

Claeys, Gregory. "Owen, Robert (1771-1858), Socialist and Philanthropist." In *Dictionary of National Biography*, edited by David Cannadine. Oxford: Oxford University Press, 2004. https://doi.org/10.1093/ref:odnb/21027.

Cliff, Tony. *Lenin*. Vol. 1, *Building the Party*. London: Pluto Press, 1975.

———. *Lenin*. Vol. 3, *Revolution Besieged*. London: Pluto Press, 1978.

Crenshaw, Kimberle. "Demarginalizing the Intersection of Race and Sex: A Black Feminist Critique of Antidiscrimination Doctrine, Feminist Theory and Antiracist Politics." *University of Chicago Legal Forum*, 1989, 139–67.

———. "Mapping the Margins: Intersectionality, Identity Politics, and Violence against Women of Color." *Stanford Law Review* 43, no. 6 (1990): 1241–99.

Dallin, David. "Between the World War and the NEP." In *The Mensheviks: From the Revolution of 1917 to the Second World War*, edited by Leopold H. Haimson, translated by Gertrude Vakar, 95–106. Inter-University Project on the History of the Menshevik Movement. Chicago: University of Chicago Press, 1974.

Dan, Lidiia Osipovna. "Sem'ia: Iz vospominanii" [The Family: Fragments from memory]. In *Martov i ego blizkie: sbornik* [Martov and his circle: A compilation], edited by L. O. Dan, B.L. Dvinov, and B. M. Sapir, 7–37. New York, 1959.

Dan, Lydia [Lidiia] Osipovna. 'Tenth Interview'. In *The Making of Three Russian Revolutionaries: Voices from the Menshevik Past*, edited by Leopold H. Haimson, 177–89. New York: Cambridge University Press, 1987.

Davis, Jonathan *Historical Dictionary of the Russian Revolution. (HDRR)*. Lanham, Maryland: Rowman & Littlefield, 2020.

Davidson, Neil. *How Revolutionary Were the Bourgeois Revolutions?* Chicago: Haymarket Books, 2012.

Deutscher, Isaac. *The Prophet Armed*. London: Oxford University Press, 1954.

Dobrovol'skii, Dmitrii, and Liudmila Peppel'. "Revoliutsiia, vosstanie, perevorot: Semantika i pragmatika" [Revolution, uprising, overturn: Semantics and pragmatics]. *Scando-Slavica* 58, no. 1 (2012): 77–100.

Docherty, J. C. *Historical Dictionary of Socialism. (HDS)*. Lanham, Maryland: Scarecrow Press, 1997.

Docherty, J. C., and Jacobus Hermanus Antonius van der Velden. *Historical Dictionary of Organized Labor. (HDOL)*. 3rd ed. Lanham, Maryland: Scarecrow Press, 2012.

Ellman, Michael. "Zasulich, Vera Ivanovna." In *Encyclopedia of Russian History*, edited by James R. Millar, 4:1720–21. New York: Macmillan Reference, 2004.

Enticott, Peter. *The Russian Liberals and the Revolution of 1905*. London: Routledge, 2016.

Figes, Orlando. *A People's Tragedy: The Russian Revolution, 1891–1924*. New York: Penguin, 1998.

Fisher, David James. *Romain Rolland and the Politics of Intellectual Engagement*. Los Angeles: University of California Press, 1988.

Fitzgerald, Edward Peter. "Émile Pouget, the Anarchist Movement, and the Origins of Revolutionary Trade-Unionism in France (1880-1901)." Ph.D., Yale University, 1973.

Getzler, Israel. *Martov: A Political Biography of a Russian Social Democrat*. Cambridge: Cambridge University Press, 1967.

Glazov, Yuri. "The Soviet Intelligentsia, Dissidents and the West." Studies in Soviet Thought 19, no. 4 (1979): 321–44.

Gramsci, Antonio. "On the L'Ordine Nuovo Programme." 1920. In *Antonio Gramsci: Selections from Political Writings 1921–1926*, edited by Quintin Hoare, translated by John Mathews, 291–98. New York: International Publishers, 1978.

Grey, Vivian. *The Chemist Who Lost His Head: The Story of Antoine Laurent Lavoisier*. New York: Coward, McCann & Geoghegan, 1982.

Guillaume, James. *L'Internationale: Documents et souvenirs (1864–1878)*. 2 vols. Paris: Société nouvelle de librairie et d'édition, 1905.

Haimson, Leopold H. *The Making of Three Russian Revolutionaries: Voices from the Menshevik Past*. New York: Cambridge University Press, 1987.

———. *The Russian Marxists and the Origins of Bolshevism*. Boston: Beacon Press, 1955.

Hanson, Paul R. *Historical Dictionary of the French Revolution*. (*HDFR*). Lanham, Maryland: Rowman & Littlefield, 2015.

Hegel, Georg Wilhelm Friedrich. "Preface to *Philosophy of Right*." In *Philosophy of Right*. Translated by S. W. Dyde, 1820. https://www. marxists.org/reference/archive/hegel/works/pr/preface.htm.

Herzen, Aleksandr. "Letter Ten (Paris, 10 June 1848)." In *Letters from France and Italy: 1847–1851*, edited and translated by Judith E. Zimmerman, 140–61. 1848. Reprint, Pittsburgh: University of Pittsburgh Press, 1995.

Hill, Christopher. *The English Revolution 1640: An Essay*. 3rd ed. 1955. Reprint, London: Lawrence & Wishart Ltd., 1979.

Jacob, Louis. *Hébert le Père Duchesne, chef des sans-culottes*. Paris: Gallimard, 1960.

Hook, Sidney. "Introduction." In Raphael R. Abramovitch, *The Soviet Revolution, 1917–1939*, vii–xii. London: George Allen and Unwin, 1962.

Institut Marksizma-Leninizma pri tsk KPSS [Institute of Marxism-Leninism of the Central Committee of the CPSU]. *Vtoroi s"ezd RSDRP Iiul'-Avgust 1903 Goda: Protokoly* [Second Congress of the RSDRP July-August 1903: Minutes]. Moscow: Gosudarstvennoe izdatel'stvo politicheskoi literatury [State publishing house of political literature], 1959.

Johnstone, Monty. "Marx, Blanqui and Majority Rule." *Socialist Register* 20 (1983): 296–318.

Kautsky, Karl. *The Dictatorship of the Proletariat*. 1918. Translated by J.L. Stenning. Manchester: National Labour Press, 1919.

———. *The Road to Power*. Translated by Algie Martin Simons. Chicago: Samuel A. Bloch, 1909.

Krupskaya, Nadezhda K. *Memories of Lenin*. Translated by E. Verney. Allahabad: India, 1930.

Lande, Nelson P. "Posthumous Rehabilitation and the Dust-Bin of History."
Public Affairs Quarterly 4, no. 3 (1990): 267–86.

Lang, Karl. "Naine, Charles." In *Biographical Dictionary of European Labor
Leaders*, edited by A. T. Lane, 2:688. Westport: Greenwood Publishing
Group, 1995.

Langewiesche, Dieter. "Revolution in Germany: Constitutional State—
Nation State—Social Reform." In *Europe in 1848: Revolution and Reform*,
edited by Dieter Dowe, Heinz-Gerhard Haupt, Dieter Langewiesche,
and Jonathan Sperber, translated by David Higgins, 120–44. Oxford:
Berghahn Books, 2001.

Lavrov, Peter Lavrovich. *Parizhskaia kommuna 18 marta 1871 goda* [The Paris
Commune of March 18, 1871]. Petrograd: Kolos, 1919.

Lenin, V. I. *Lenin: Collected Works.* (*LCW*). 45 vols. Translation of the
fourth, enlarged Russian edition. Moscow: Progress Publishers, 1960–70.

———. *Polnoe sobranie sochinenii* [Complete collected works]. (*PSS*). Fifth
edition. 5th ed. 55 vols. Moscow: Politizdat, 1958–65.

———. *The State and Revolution: Marxist Teaching on the State and the Task
of the Proletariat in the Revolution.* London: British Socialist Party, 1919.

Lenin, V. I., and G. V. Plekhanov. "Proekt osobogo mneniia po delu N. E.
Baumana" [Draft dissenting opinion in the N.E. Bauman case]. 1902. In
Neizvestnye dokumenty, 1891-1922 [Unknown documents, 1891-1922], by
Vladimir Il'ich Lenin, 427. Moscow: ROSSPEN (Russian State Archive
of Social and Political History), 2000.

Levi, Paul. "Our Path: Against Putschism." 1921. In *In the Steps of Rosa
Luxemburg: Selected Writings of Paul Levi*, edited by David Fernbach,
Historical Materialism Book Series, 31, 119–65. 1921. Leiden: Brill, 2011.

Lewis, Ben, ed. *Martov and Zinoviev: Head to Head in Halle.* London:
November Publications, 2011.

———. "The four-hour speech and the significance of Halle." In *Martov
and Zinoviev: Head to Head in Halle*, edited by Ben Lewis, 7-38. London:
November Publications, 2011.

Liebich, André. *From the Other Shore: Russian Social Democracy after 1921.*
Harvard Historical Studies 125. Cambridge, Mass: Harvard University
Press, 1997.

Lih, Lars T. *Lenin Rediscovered: What Is to Be Done? in Context.* Historical
Materialism Book Series, 9. Leiden: Brill, 2006.

———. "Martov in Halle." In *Martov and Zinoviev: Head to Head in Halle*, edited by Ben Lewis, 161–65. London: November Publications, 2011.

Loughlin, Michael B. "Gustave Hervé's Transition from Socialism to National Socialism: Continuity and Ambivalence." *Journal of Contemporary History* 38, no. 4 (2003): 515–38.

Louis, Paul. *Histoire du socialisme français*. Paris: Éditions de la Revue Blanche, 1901.

Luxemburg, Rosa. "The Mass Strike, the Political Party, and the Trade Union." 1906. In *The Essential Rosa Luxemburg: Reform or Revolution and the Mass Strike*, edited by Helen Scott, 111–82. Chicago: Haymarket Books, 2007.

———. "The Russian Revolution." (1918). In *The Rosa Luxemburg Reader*, 281-310. Edited by Peter Hudis and Kevin Anderson. Translated by Bertram D. Wolfe. New York: Monthly Review Press, 2004.

———. "Social Reform or Revolution" (1899). In *The Rosa Luxemburg Reader*, 128–67. Edited by Peter Hudis and Kevin Anderson. Translated by Dick Howard. New York: Monthly Review Press, 2004.

Mandel, David. *The Petrograd Workers and the Fall of Old Regime: From the February Revolution to the July Days, 1917*. Basingstoke: Macmillan Press, 1983.

Margulis, Alexander, and Asya Kholodnaya. *Russian-English Dictionary of Proverbs and Sayings*. London: McFarland & Company Inc., 2000.

Markus, V. and R. Senkus. "Kharkiv." *Encyclopedia of Ukraine*, 441–49. Toronto: University of Toronto Press, 1988.2006.

Martov, Iulii. *Izbrannoe* [Selected Works]. Edited by S. V. Tyutyukin, O. V. Volobuev, and I. Kh. Urilov. Moscow: s.n., 2000.

———. *Mirovoi bol'shevizm* [World Bolshevism]. Edited by Fedor Dan. Berlin: Spark, 1923.

———. "The Roots of World Bolshevism." In *Mysl'* [Thought], [Journal article]. 1919. Marxists Internet Archive, 2008. https://www.marxists. org/archive/martov/1919/xx/worldbolsh.html.

———. "The State and the Socialist Revolution." In *What Next?*, translated by Integer [Herman Jerson]. 1919. http://www.whatnextjournal.org.uk/ Pages/Theory/Articles.html, n.d.

———. *The State and the Socialist Revolution*. Translated by Integer [Herman Jerson]. 1919. New York: International Review, 1938.

Marx, Karl. *On History and People*. Edited by Saul K. Padover. Karl Marx Library, v. 7. New York; McGraw-Hill, 1977.

―――. "Marx über Feuerbach" [Theses on Feuerbach]. 1845. In *Gesamtausgabe (MEGA)*, by Karl Marx and Friedrich Engels, 792–94. edited by Friedrich Engels. Karl Marx Friedrich Engels Gesamtausgabe (MEGA). Berlin: Akadamie Verlag, 2011.

Marx, Karl, and Frederick Engels. *Marx/Engels Collected Works*. 50 vols. (*MECW*). London: Lawrence and Wishart, 1976–2004.

Mehring, Franz. *Karl Marx: The Story of His Life*. Translated by Edward Fitzgerald. 1918. Reprint, Ann Arbor: University of Michigan Press, 1962.

Meisel, James H. "A Premature Fascist?—Sorel and Mussolini." *Western Political Quarterly* 3, no. 1 (March 1950): 14–27. https://doi.org/10.1177/106591295000300102.

Melgunov, S. P. *The Bolshevik Seizure of Power*. Edited by Sergei G. Pushkarev. Translated by James S. Beaver. Translation and Abridgement of S. P. Mel'gunov *Kak bol'sheviki zakhvatili vlast'* [How the bolsheviks seized power]. Paris: La Renaissance, 1953. Santa Barbara, Calif., 1972.

Merriman, John M. *The Dynamite Club: How a Bombing in Fin-de-Siècle Paris Ignited the Age of Modern Terror*. New Haven: Yale University Press, 2016.

Miéville, China. *October: The Story of the Russian Revolution*. London: Verso, 2017.

Molière. "George Dandin ou le mari confondu." In *Théâtre complet, 1622–1673*, 1–59. 1668. Reprint, Paris: Librairie de France, 1923.

Morgan, David W. *The Socialist Left and the German Revolution: A History of the German Independent Social Democratic Party, 1917-1922*. Ithaca, NY: Cornell University Press, 1975.

Mühlestein, Hans. "Marx and the Utopian Wilhelm Weitling." *Science & Society* 12, no. 1 (1948): 113–29.

Naine, Charles. *Dictature du prolétariat ou démocratie*. Lausanne: Imprimerie populaire, 1918.

Naarden, Bruno. *Socialist Europe and Revolutionary Russia: Perception and Prejudice, 1848–1923*. Cambridge: Cambridge University Press, 2002.

"News from Russia." *The Russian Review* 1, no. 4 (May 1916): 247–49.

Nil'skii, Mikhail [Ivan Mitrofanovich Khoroshev]. *Vorkuta*. Samizdat [self-published, underground] edition, 1986.

O'Brien, Mark. *Perish the Privileged Orders: A Socialist History of the Chartist Movement*. London: Redwords, 1995.

Orlovskii, P. "Kommunisticheskii Internatsional i Mirovaia Sovetskaia Respublika" [The Communist International and the World Soviet Republic]. *Pravda*, no. 101 (13 May 1919): 1.

Ovtcharenko, Claude, ed. "Déclaration au people Français." In *Journal officiel de la Commune de Paris du 20 mars au 24 mai 1871*, 2005. http:// classiques.uqac.ca/classiques/commune_de_paris/Journal_officiel_ Commune_de_Paris/Journal_officiel_Commune_de_Paris.html.

Owen, Robert. *A New View of Society and Other Writings*. 1813. Reprint, New York: E.P. Dutton & Co. Inc., 1922.

Pippin, Robert. "Hegel's Practical Philosophy: The Realization of Freedom." In *The Cambridge Companion to German Idealism*, edited by Karl Ameriks, 180–99. Cambridge: Cambridge University Press, 2000

Pliny the Elder. *Pliny's Natural History, in Thirty-Seven Books*. Translated by Philemon Holland. London: Wernerian Club, 1847–48.

Potressov [Potresov], Alexander. "Lenin: Versuch einer Charakterisierung" [Lenin: An Attempt at a Characterization]. *Die Gesellschaft: Internationale Revue für Sozialismus und Politik* 4, no. 2 (1927): 405–18.

Pouget, Émile. *La Confédération générale du travail*. Paris: Librairie des Sciences Politiques et Sociales, 1908.

Rees, Arthur D. "An Interpretation of Slavophilism." *The Scientific Monthly* 1, no. 1 (1915): 47–55.

Rossiiskaia sotsial-demokraticheskaia rabochaia partiia [Russian Social Democratic Labour Party]. *1903, Second Ordinary Congress of the RSDLP: Complete Text of the Minutes*. Translated by Brian Pearce. London: New Park Publications, 1978.

Rule, John. "Morrison, James (1802–1835), Journalist and Trade Unionist." In *Oxford Dictionary of National Biography*, edited by David Cannadine. Oxford, Oxford University Press, 2004. https://doi.org/10.1093/ ref:odnb/48765.

Ryan, Barbara. "Personal Is Political." *Blackwell Encyclopedia of Sociology* (online edition). 31 December 2013. https://doi. org/10.1002/9781405165518.wbeosp018.pub2.

Savel'ev, P. Iu, and S. V. Tiutiukin. "Iulii Osipovich Martov (1873–1923): The Man and the Politician." *Russian Studies in History* 45, no. 1 (1 June 2006): 6–92.

Saville, John. "JE Smith and the Owenite Movement, 1833-1834." In *Robert Owen, Prophet of the Poor: Essays in Honour of the Two Hundredth Anniversary of His Birth*, edited by Sidney Pollard and John Salt, 115–44. London: The Macmillan Press Ltd., 1971.

Schiller, Friedrich. "Fiesco; or, the Genoese Conspiracy." In *Schiller's Complete Works*, edited and translated by Charles J. Hempel, 203–40. Philadelphia: I. Kohler, 1861.

Schönhoven, Klaus. "Heckert, Fritz." In *Biographical Dictionary of European Labor Leaders*, edited by A. T. Lane, 1:412. Westport: Greenwood Publishing Group, 1995.

Scott, Helen. "Introduction to Rosa Luxemburg." In *The Essential Rosa Luxemburg: Reform or Revolution and the Mass Strike*, by Rosa Luxemburg, 1–36. edited by Helen Scott. Chicago: Haymarket Books, 2007.

Seignobos, Charles. "La troisième république." In *Le monde contemporain, 1870–1900*, vol. 12 of *Histoire générale du IVe siècle à nos jours*, edited by Ernest Lavisse and Alfred Rambaud, 2nd ed., 1–51.

Senn, Alfred Erich. "The Politics of *Golos* and *Nashe Slovo*." *International Review of Social History* 17, no. 2 (1972): 675–704.

Serge, Victor. "A Letter and Some Notes." *The New International* 5, no. 2 (February 1939): 53–54.

———. *Memoirs of a Revolutionary*. Translated by Peter Sedgwick with George Paizis. New York: New York Review Books, 2012. Originally published as *Mémoires d'un révolutionnaire de 1901 à 1941* (Paris: Éditions du Seuil, 1951).

Simmel, Georg. "The Triad." In *The Sociology of Georg Simmel*, edited and translated by Kurt H. Wolff, 145–69. 1908. Reprint, Glencoe, IL: The Free Press, 1950.

Soboul, Albert. *Précis d'histoire de la révolution française*. Paris: Editions Sociales, 1962.

———. *The Sans-Culottes: The Popular Movement and Revolutionary Government, 1793-1794*. Princeton, NJ: Princeton University Press, 1980.

Stunt, Timothy C. F. "Smith, James Elishama [Called Shepherd Smith]." In *Oxford Dictionary of National Biography*, edited by David Cannadine. Oxford: Oxford University Press, 2004. http://www.oxforddnb.com/view/article/25826.

Sukhanov, N. N. [Nikolai Nikolaevich]. *The Russian Revolution, 1917: A Personal Record.* 1922-23. Edited, abridged, and translated by Joel Carmichael. 1922. Princeton, NJ: Princeton University Press, 1984.

———. *Zapiski o revoliutsii* [Notes on the revolution]. Vol. 7. 7 vols. Berlin, Petersburg, Moscow: Izdatel'stvo E. I. Grizhebina, 1922.

Surya, Michel. *Georges Bataille: An Intellectual Biography.* London: Verso, 2002.

Taylor, Miles. "O'Brien, James [Pseud. Bronterre O'Brien] (1804–1864), Chartist." In *Oxford Dictionary of National Biography,* edited by David Cannadine. Oxford: Oxford University Press, 2004. https://doi.org/10.1093/ref:odnb/20457.

Tosstorff, Reiner. *The Red International of Labour Unions (RILU) 1920 - 1937.* Translated by Ben Fowkes. Historical Materialism Book Series. Leiden: Brill, 2016.

Tridon, Gustave. *Gironde et Girondins. La Gironde en 1869 et en 1793.* Paris: Dufour et Ce, 1869.

Trotsky, Leon. *The History of the Russian Revolution.* Vol. 3, *The Triumph of the Soviets.* Translated by Max Eastman. 1930. Reprint, New York: Simon and Schuster, 1937.

———. *Nashi politicheskie zadachi (takticheskie i organizatsionnye voprosy)* [Our political tasks (tactical and organisational questions)]. Geneva: Rossiiskoi Sotsialdemokraticheskoi Rabochii Partii, 1904.

———. *Our Political Tasks.* London: New Park Publications, 1979. First published 1904 in Russian.

———. *Politicheskie siluety* [Political profiles]. Vol. 8 of Leon Trotsky, *Sochineniia* [Works], edited by I. M. Pavlov. Moscow: Gosizdat, 1926.

———. *The Revolution Betrayed.* 1937. New York: Pathfinder Press, 1973.

Tsutsiev, Arthur. "Administrative Units of the Russian Empire and the USSR." In *Atlas of the Ethno-Political History of the Caucasus,* translated by Nora Seligman Favorov, 195–203. New Haven: Yale University Press, 2014.

Walker, David M., and Daniel Gray. *Historical Dictionary of Marxism.* (*HDM*) Lanham, Maryland: Scarecrow Press, 2007.

Weill, Georges. "Philippe Buonarroti (1761-1837)." *Revue Historique* 76, no. 2 (1901): 241–75.

Weitling, Wilhelm. "Letter by Wilhelm Weitling to Moses Hess." 31 March 1846. *Marx/Engels Archive*, https://www.marxists.org/archive/marx/works/1847/communist-league/1846let1.htm.

White, James D. *Lenin: The Practice and Theory of Revolution*. New York: Palgrave, 2001.

Wieczynski, Joseph L., ed. *The Modern Encyclopedia of Russian and Soviet History*. (*MERSH*) 55 vols. Gulf Breeze, Fl: Academic International Press, 1976-1993.

Wittke, Carl Frederick. *The Utopian Communist; a Biography of Wilhelm Weitling, Nineteenth-Century Reformer*. Baton Rouge: Louisiana State University Press, 1950.

Wolin, Simon. "The Mensheviks under the NEP and in Emigration." In *The Mensheviks: From the Revolution of 1917 to the Second World War*, edited by Leopold H. Haimson, translated by Gertrude Vakar, 241-348. Inter-University Project on the History of the Menshevik Movement. Chicago: University of Chicago Press, 1974.

Zinoviev, Grigory. "Twelve Days in Germany." (1921) In *Martov and Zinoviev: Head to Head in Halle*, edited by Ben Lewis, translated by CPGB, 7-38. London: November Publications, 2011.

Index

Dallin, David, 8, 9

Dan, Fedor, 8, 129n25

Dan, Lidiia Osipovna, 17, 132n57

Dandin, George, 57

Däumig, Ernest, 77–78, 149n22

De Leon, Daniel, 103, 158n37

democracy: Bolshevik state's view
of, 4, 5; its relationship to
dictatorship of proletariat,
95–96, 123, 124; and the Paris
Commune, 96–97; Plekhanov's
view on limits of, 147n15,
154n25; proletarians' problem
with, 91–94; soviet structure
of political organization and,
60–61, 71–74; in Tsarist Russia,
147n16

dictatorship of a minority: how it
developed in France, 80–81; how
it developed in Russia, 68–69;
and materialism, 81–84; in
revolutions of earlier era, 69–70;
in Switzerland, 81

dictatorship of the bourgeoisie, 98

dictatorship of the proletariat
(*see also* new proletariat): and
development of proletariat
between 1848 and 1871,
119–20; effect of Blanquism
on Marx's view of, 115–16;
essential condition of, 98; how
it develops, 63; Marx's hope for
in Paris Commune, 120–23;
relationship of democracy to,
91–97; RSDRP program for,
124; as social character of state

power, 97; temporary victories
before accomplishing, 117–18

Dunoyer (witness of Paris
Commune), 107

Ebert, Friedrich, 137n7

Engels, Friedrich: belief in
democratic values of Paris
Commune, 96–97; changed
view of revolution for, 116; on
consciousness and revolution,
64; on development of
dictatorship of proletariat,
95–97; how dictatorship mixes
with democracy, 123; how his
view of state power changed,
112; importance of overthrow
of military-bureaucratic state
machine to, 94–95, 98, 109,
154n21; influence of Blanquism
on, 115–16, 162n2; K. Marx
correspondence with, 108;
necessary precedents for
dictatorship of proletariat, 98;
R. Luxemburg on his view of
proletarian power, 115; seen
as statist, 107; view of 1848
revolution, 119; view of England,
94; view of proletariat in 1871, 122

England, 46, 47, 93–94

English Revolution, 140n17

Erfurt program, 95, 154n19

European socialism, 41–42, 53, 54, 76

federalism, 66–67, 102–4

federation of communes, 102–7

Finland, 42, 137n5